Tea and Tortillas

´Start enjoying your life – by moving abroad´

Stuart Wright

Synopsis

Sometimes, what appears at first sight to be an unmitigated disaster can give rise to a fantastic opportunity. Often, times of change and upheaval force us to reconsider what it is we want out of life, to take a rain check and think perhaps, as Stuart did, 'Do I really want to live in the UK any more?'

Even if you lose your job but are pretty sure you'll be able to get another one, you may decide that you want more out of life than simply carrying on doing what you've always done, at the mercy of an ever-changing economy that sweeps you along on a continuous cycle of boom and bust over which you have no control. And if you're lucky enough to have been given a redundancy cheque or contract pay-off, now could be the time to make your dream of living abroad a reality.

Stuart and his wife Christine had a large house in Yorkshire, well-paid jobs and a good lifestyle – everything anyone could wish for. Except that Stuart was spending hours in the car every week, rushing up and down the motorway to and from work. And one day he decided he'd had enough. So, Stuart and Chris sold everything and moved to Spain – and a few months later, they were running an English teashop on the Costa del Sol, with customers ranging from the mildly eccentric to the downright weird, from the naïve to the mind-blowingly infuriating, who provided Stuart with a wealth of material for this amusing and informative book.

Retiring to the sun is a dream shared by many of the hundreds of thousands of Brits who have had holidays abroad. But around every corner there lurks an unscrupulous wheeler-dealer waiting to part the trusting and unwary from their hard-earned cash, and the potential hazards and pitfalls are virtually limitless.

Tea & Tortillas is a humorous, easy-to-read book about the realities of living in Spain, and provides all the information anyone could need about renting or buying property, getting a 'proper job', buying and running a business, the Spanish culture, and much, much more. It is also very funny!

So, if you're desperate to make a fresh start somewhere completely different, or are thinking of jumping off the UK hamster wheel for any reason - read on!

Contents

Preface

During the first few months I lived in Spain, I couldn't believe some of the things I saw and heard. Nothing specific, it was just wacky listening to some people. After a year, you think you've seen it all and heard it all, but there we go again, some more twaddle. You never stop being surprised by some of the scams that go on and some of the complete rubbish you listen to from Brits living in Spain – and from some Spaniards too. 'Never take people at face value.' That's a true statement wherever you live, but down here you couldn't do that even if you were prepared to.

It's true that 'Many very rich people move to Spain and go home rich.' (You might need to read that again.) And it's also true that many not so rich people move over here from the UK and go home absolutely and utterly broke. They move to Spain, leave their brains on the plane, jump straight in with both feet and don't think things through. They trust people they shouldn't trust, and they lose everything. It's very sad, but unfortunately it's not unusual.

The number of times I said to Chris, 'You could write a book about this lot.' In fact, I said it so many times that I did write a book, and here it is. It's an account of my own experiences and my observation of others, a light-hearted, layman's view of life on the Costa del Sol. But it also contains some very good advice.

There are so many traps you can fall into over here, and so many frustrations. Trying to get anything done can be a mammoth task – like walking through treacle. All too often, Brits get it completely wrong and their dream life turns into a horror film. The main reason that British people often fail when they move to Spain is the old 'fools rush in' syndrome. The best advice I could offer to anyone who is considering moving down here is to come over first for an extended holiday, the longer the better, in order to look, listen and learn. There's a lot to learn. If you come with an 'I know everything' attitude, you'll inevitably get bombed from a great height. There's someone on every street corner waiting to take your money away from you, and many succeed – and a good proportion of these people are Brits themselves.

There isn't the legal protection in Spain that's taken for granted in the UK, and for some people scruples do not exist.

I am certainly not an academic, but I like to think I'm a fairly quick learner, and I am a good observer. This book covers a number of topics that are drawn from my own experiences. Like anyone else, I have made mistakes. But if by writing this book I can save other people from making the same mistakes, I will have achieved something. I wish the information in this book had been available to me prior to moving to Spain. I would, without a doubt, have saved a fortune.

—

Chapter 1
A lot isn't always enough

Faster, faster, like a hamster in its wheel, running just to stand still. It's the norm isn't it, in the UK? That's how I saw myself for the last few years of my working life in England – as a hamster in a wheel.

My wife Chris and I had a very good lifestyle. We lived near the moors above Halifax, in a large detached house with a huge garden at the end of a private drive, on which stood two new cars. We could eat out more or less whenever and wherever we chose, and had at least two decent holidays a year. Life was good. We worked hard for it though, very hard indeed.

More often than not, we spent our two main holidays each year on the smaller Greek islands, usually choosing the ones you couldn't fly to directly, as the fewer people we saw on holiday the better. Not that we were anti-social by any means, but we enjoy each other's company, and two weeks of doing absolutely nothing together was our idea of paradise.

Chris also went for the occasional long weekend to Fuengirola to visit her children from a previous marriage, Jonathan and Justine, who had lived on the Costa del Sol for a number of years. Jonathan had moved there first and got into selling timeshares, and then Justine followed some time later, lured by the appeal of her brother's life in the sun. Although I'd occasionally join Chris on her trips to Spain, when my work permitted, Fuengirola was never a place we considered going to for our 'proper' holidays, as there are too many people there and it seemed too commercialised for our liking. But, on the other hand, having the sun on our backs made up for a lot, wherever we were.

I was the sales director of a large, Leeds-based printed packaging company, and Chris ran the accounts department at a road haulage company on the outskirts of Bradford. For most of the last couple of years of the time I was based in Leeds, I'd been flying all over the place. I did a lot of business in Saudi Arabia and Morocco, with occasional trips to Egypt and North Yemen, and when the company I was working for set out on the acquisition trail, I also started travelling to its newly acquired companies in the UK, France and Holland. When I went into my local pub on a Friday evening, friends would ask, 'Where have you been jetting away to this week then, Stuart?' and my answer of 'Paris', 'Amsterdam', 'Cairo' or wherever would bring the response, 'You lucky bugger. What a life you have!'

It sounds great doesn't it? And, to start with, it is, but after a while you get absolutely sick of the loneliness and of spending hours in airports and eating in hotels. I could fly to Paris in the morning and be back the same evening, which sounds quite exciting, but I hadn't actually seen anything apart from the airport, the inside of a couple of taxis and the office I was visiting. Believe me, it's not as great as it may seem.

Then the company I worked for made a major acquisition in the form of our biggest competitor, a company at Hinckley in Leicestershire that had an annual turnover well in excess of £20 million and was haemorrhaging huge amounts of money every month. The main board of directors brought in directors from different disciplines within the existing group with a view to analysing the business, restructuring it and turning it around, and I was asked to be the sales director for what would probably be about a year.

The people at Hinckley were great; the directors, managers and staff worked very hard indeed on what was an incredibly difficult task, and I really enjoyed the challenge of my new position. Parts of the business were moved to other sites within the group, and other parts of the group were moved in, and eventually my one year stint turned into three years when I was asked to take on the job on a permanent basis. So, for most days over the next three years, I commuted from our home near Halifax to Hinckley – a round trip of 240 miles. I drove up and down the motorway until I swear I knew every signpost and lamppost on that stretch of the M1. But it was worth it, because during our first full financial year we made a very small profit (pennies), which was one hell of an achievement considering the huge losses when we took the business over.

But the other side of the coin was that those three years were complete hell in terms of travelling and the amount of time I was away from home. Chris was very supportive, but, understandably, she wasn't at all happy with a situation that began as a temporary position and turned into a permanent job. After the first two years, we considered moving to Leicestershire, and looked at various properties in and around Market Bosworth. But fortunately we didn't buy. Around that time, a major retailer that was very important to our company was making loud noises about moving large chunks of its printed packaging business overseas. My instincts told me that something wasn't quite right, so I suggested to Chris that we put the proposed relocation on ice for a while – and, sure enough, the business was taken away from us, and as it represented a very significant chunk of our revenue, the writing was on the wall and it looked unlikely that the company would survive. We were shafted, as the fixed overheads of our factory were huge and even major surgery on the head count wasn't going to make things any better.

Every avenue was explored, from downsizing to a sale to breaking the company up, but none of the numbers stacked up. So the decision was made to close the plant, and every employee would have to go. That meant around 250 people – good people – losing their jobs. What a waste! Three directors, including myself and the commercial manager, were retained for a further three months in order to pull as much cash back as possible by chasing debts and selling stock, raw materials and machinery. You name it and we tried to flog it.

We were on an 'earn-out' bonus and it was an opportunity to generate good money, because, as I'd been with the company for more than 20 years in total, and a director for 12 years, the money they'd have to pay me was significant. I could have stayed with the company and gone back to Leeds, and had been offered jobs on the same or even more money, but my mind had started to wander.

Then, one evening, after my usual trip up the M1, I drove my new Saab up our drive, turned off the engine, slid down into the soft leather seats and closed my eyes. I was doing at least 1,500 miles a week, getting home at 8.30 in the evening, eating the lovely meal Chris had prepared for me, knocking back a quick gin and tonic, if I was lucky, and falling asleep. As I sat there, the thought struck me like a sudden revelation: 'Sack this. I just don't want to do it any more! Why don't we move to the sun and enjoy life?' Well, why not? We're only here once, as far as we know, and there had to be other, more enjoyable things I could be spending my life doing.

I started to think about the fat pay slip nestled safely in my pocket. It was certainly a decent amount of money to earn in a month, but in fact about half of it went to other people, not least the Chancellor. I began to do the sums.

Gross pay x

Net pay y

Gross pay – net pay $\mathbf{Z}$

Who the hell gets the not insignificant amount represented by $\mathbf{Z}$ then? I can't ever recall seeing the Chancellor on the M1 at 5.30 in the morning.

I sat there in the car for about 20 minutes, just thinking, and then went into the house and, somewhat hesitantly, told Chris my thoughts over a gin and tonic or ten. I didn't really know how to raise the subject, because I was sure she'd think I'd gone completely insane. Give all this up? Why? But Chris and I are great mates, and her reaction was something along the lines of, 'Well it's a huge step, but let's talk it through and consider it.'

After that, we sat down night after night and discussed the best way forward, until we finally decided just to go for it. We'd sell our house and move to the sun. If it didn't work out, as long as we'd protected our capital, we'd just return to the UK and jump back onto the old hamster wheel again. It was an exciting prospect: an adventure and a dream. I remember one evening saying jokingly to Chris that I felt like a pioneer, and as I made the comment I suddenly remembered something my old boss, Hugh Donaldson, once said to me: 'Shit,' I said to Chris. 'The pioneers are usually the ones who return with arrows in their backs!'

We had to think it all through thoroughly; it was going to be a massive step, and we had to do absolutely everything in our power to ensure that our dream didn't turn into a nightmare.

First of all we had to decide where to go. Living on one of our beloved Greek islands would be the ultimate, wouldn't it? Well actually, probably not. Tourists see these tiny Greek islands whilst on holiday in the summer, when they are nothing short of paradise. But in the winter, many of the local inhabitants either go to Athens to drive taxis or disappear into the hills and mountains to pick olives, which means that many of the picture postcard coastal villages are virtually deserted during the winter months. And there's no airport. Let's just imagine for a moment getting something like appendicitis in December – you'd probably die. Seriously!

So that was lesson number 1: going on holiday to the sun and moving permanently to the sun involve completely different considerations and priorities. We would have to think about infrastructure, medical facilities, winter climate, banks and much more.

We considered just about everywhere you can think of, and when we listed all the things we wanted, common sense told us that the Costa del Sol was the place to go. Chris's children were already there, so it was the logical move to make.

Decision made, we would move to southern Spain.

Chapter 2
Selling the hamster wheel

What about the dog? We couldn't leave him; he was part of the family. We got him from the battered dogs' home at Adel near Leeds, the result of a typical children's scam. My son Oliver, who was around ten years old at the time, said, 'Yes Dad, of course I will take him out for regular walks and really look after him.' Yeah right! We named him Dino – if it was good enough for Fred Flintstone, then it was good enough for us.

When we chose him, he was the one sitting at the back of his cage cowering while the other dogs were jumping up and down barking and generally going mental. Dino had apparently previously been in the hands of drug addicts on an estate near Leeds, and the poor creature had cigarette burns on his nose and all down his left front leg. I still can't even begin to understand how a human being can treat an animal in that way. It makes you wonder which of them more deserves the title 'animal'.

The dogs' home reckoned he was 11 months old, which seemed rather specific, but who were we to argue. He was a typical five-bob mongrel, black with a white chest, but he had a wonderful temperament. We paid around a tenner for him, but after we'd collected him, we went straight to a pet shop and spent around £100 on a basket, bowls, and all the other things you need when you own a dog.

Job done – in fact, as it worked out, it was 'jobby done'!

I'd taken delivery of a very nice, brand new BMW three weeks prior to this dog episode in our lives, and Oliver was sitting proudly on the back seat with Dino, while I drove along basking in the warm glow of touchy-feely contentment at the thought of how we were about to transform the life of this lovely, badly treated little dog. Then, when we were about two miles away from our house, all hell broke loose, with Oliver and Chris shouting, 'Stop! The dogs crapped all over the back seat' – information it proved unnecessary to mention, as an unbelievably strong smell permeated throughout the car. Making an emergency stop that any driving test examiner would be impressed by, I banged my head on the steering wheel in complete panic.

What the hell have we done? How on earth can I take customers out in a shit machine, let alone drive it a couple of hundred miles myself tomorrow. There was nothing for it but to get home as soon as possible and forgive him. I don't like a car that's dirty on the outside, but when it looks like the toilet in a students' flat on the inside, and I'm the one who's going to have to clean it, with one hand covering my nose as I try to avoid throwing up, then… But what could I say? I'd grow to love Dino; I was sure I would.

Needless to say, Oliver only ever took Dino out for a walk about twice!

Preparations for the move continued, and, added to all the other things that had to be done, Chris began sorting out the dog ready for his new life abroad: injections, an electronic chip implant and everything else needed for his dog passport. Can't be bad can it: one minute the battered dogs' home near Leeds, the next, retirement on the Costa del Sol!

Once our important decision had been taken, everything moved into gear quickly, too quickly really. Our house went on the market and sold within a few days, which put the fear of god into us and helped concentrate our minds on what was really about to happen, and we sold some, but not much, of our furniture. We'd already made the decision not to jump straight into the Spanish property market; we'd rent for at least a year and, ideally, get something unfurnished so that we could have our own furniture around us. Having had a good lifestyle in the UK, we didn't want to rent a furnished property and feel like we'd gone back to a teenage bed-sit lifestyle. In fact, from what I'd seen of some of the furnished properties, it would be more like living in a set from 'The Young Ones'. Obviously you get what you pay for, but we'd been unanimous in our decision that having our own furniture around us was a must.

We then proceeded to sell off all the other things that would be surplus to requirements, including a large garden water feature, a petrol lawn mower, a 'hardly used' multi-gym and various carpets. We gave ourselves about five weeks from the time our house was sold to organise everything, which wasn't really long enough. The people who bought our house wanted to move in almost immediately, and, although that didn't suit us, we agreed rather than risk losing the sale. So a removal company duly arrived to pack everything up, and then took it into storage until we were ready to have it transported to their depot in Fuengirola.

So far so good; but where were we going to live for the next four or five weeks? It would be impossible to rent a house or flat for such a short period of time, and it would cost an absolute fortune to live in a hotel. Fortunately, a guy called Phil McGuire, who we knew from our local pub, had recently bought a very large old pub in Sowerby Bridge, which he'd had converted into very nice, very high quality, 'yuppie' flats – all glass, chrome and stainless steel with polished floors. Although Phil rented the apartments out for long-term lets, he kindly let us have one for four weeks, right up to our day of departure for Spain.

Meanwhile my company car went back, which was a sad moment for me, and that left just one more piece of the jigsaw missing. I had been a scooter boy in my teens and had owned a couple of beautiful, fully chromed-up Lambrettas, but since then I'd always yearned for a Harley Davidson motorbike. When you're younger, you can't afford something like that, and when you can afford one, you're in grave danger of looking like some sad old git trying to relive his youth. I'd already broached the subject with Chris and, as usual, she was great: 'You've earned it. Go and get one.' Yippee!

I went down to the Harley dealership in Leeds as excited as a schoolboy getting his first bike. By sheer fluke, they had on display a brand new Sportster Custom 1200 in pearlescent blue and silver, which was one of the colours I'd chosen and which I was more than happy to have as I knew that, because of the time factor involved, I wasn't in a position to place a factory order for a specific colour. My heart raced as I almost ran to the bike to stop anyone getting to it before me, and a few minutes later I was sitting down with the salesman to complete the relevant paperwork.

It was a Monday, and the guy said I could collect the bike on the Friday. 'I'm sorry,' I told him, 'but you'll have to deliver it to my house near Halifax.' He looked confused. 'Deliver it?' he said. 'Why?' 'Err, because I can't drive a motorbike.' Even if you've never been in a Harley Davidson dealership, I'm sure you can imagine that some of the people who work in them are huge, hairy, hard-arse Hell's Angel types, and this guy just stared at me with a look on his face that said, quite clearly, 'You tosser!'

It's true: I couldn't actually drive a motorbike. I'd passed the motorcycle test on one of my scooters during my teens, and it would have been perfectly legal for me to drive that 1200 cc Harley straight out of the showroom. But if I had done, I'd probably have killed myself – and half the population of Leeds – on my way home. I didn't even know how to operate the foot change gears. But with the paper work duly signed and clenched in his enormous mitts, 'Hairy Biker Man' obviously felt prepared to make allowances, and agreed to deliver the Harley to my house on the Friday as requested.

I immediately booked a one-to-one course with a motorcycle driving instructor, which cost me but brought me up to road standard in no time, and then arranged for the removal company to return and collect my new prized possession so that the bike could be shipped out to Spain with the furniture.

With everything else arranged, we decided, mainly due to Dino, that rather than fly to our new life in the sun, we'd go by car. The plan was to drive to Plymouth, catch the ferry to Santander, and then drive down through Spain. My car had already gone, but we'd bought Chris a brand new Ford Ka only a few months prior to making our decision to 'clock off'. So, although not really our vehicle of choice – not least because the steering wheel was on the wrong side – it would do for Chris, the dog and me. Chris had never liked the air-con in my cars and always chose hers with a sunroof instead, which wasn't going to be great in the Spanish climate, but we planned to drive it to Spain and then keep it going for as long as we could. Another important factor in our decision was that the car was only about six months old, so we'd lose a fortune if we sold it with no part exchange allowance.

But, as it happened, just two weeks before we were due to set sail, I was driving past our local VW/Audi dealership just outside Halifax when I spotted on the forecourt a one-year-old, new-shape VW Beetle 2.0i. When they first launched this car onto the UK market you could only buy left-hand drive, which was what this one was. It must have been fate; it was obviously meant to be, except perhaps for one thing – the car was in a sort of baby-sick lime green. Still, you can't have everything. So I veered into the garage, did a deal on a swap for the Ford Ka, and we were all set to drive to Spain in a left-hand-drive car, albeit a daft-looking Beetle that would probably only really appeal to a particularly flamboyant hairdresser.

On the day of our departure, we took Dino to the vet for his final check-up and to get his dog passport, and then drove to Plymouth via

Bath. I've always loved the City of Bath and Chris had never been there, so I'd booked us into a hotel that accepted dogs and we arrived in the late afternoon and had a wander round and then a meal in a nice restaurant, and a few beers. Well, quite a lot of beers actually. Next morning we had another wander round and then jumped into the car and set off for Plymouth where, again, I'd booked us into a dog-friendly hotel. But this time it was an early night, as the ferry left at 9.00 in the morning.

We'd booked a cabin for the 24-hour crossing, as we didn't relish the thought of trying to sleep on one of those aircraft-type seats surrounded by screaming kids and pissed-up lunatics. I was pretty sure there'd be pissed-up lunatics on board, as I seem to remember being one of them myself once on a trip to a Belgian beer festival – and on the way back again!

Dino had to stay in the car for the duration of the crossing. When we'd booked the ferry, we'd been told that dog owners could go to their cars every three hours and walk their dogs for ten minutes. I'd assumed, wrongly as it turned out, that a crew member would accompany dogs and their owners around the deck, but what actually happens is that a crew member unlocks the door to your particular car deck and you can walk your dog around that. If you've ever been on a car ferry, you'll know that the cars are packed in so tightly that there's barely enough space between them for the severely anorexic. What you may not have noticed, however, is that the floors on some decks are not solid; they're similar to the top deck of a road car transporter. You can probably see where this is leading! As the floor has holes in it, the chances are that when your dog goes to the toilet, whatever comes out drops onto the deck below, which in reality means onto the roof of a car, or, worse still, onto a roof rack full of luggage! Next time you take a Cabriolet onto a ferry, look up – or perhaps don't!

All credit to Dino: every time I went down to walk him, I had a vision of the mess that might confront me on the lime green and yellow seats, but he managed to keep his bodily functions under control between toilet breaks. We were lucky. There were several cars with large dogs in them, and some with more than one, and there must have been some far less fortunate people whose cars looked like a muck spreader had travelled through them by the end of the 24-hour crossing.

Finally, we arrived at Santander and set off to drive almost non-stop to Fuengirola, with the occasional petrol and toilet break. The car was loaded to bursting point and every time we stopped and opened a door, half the stuff fell out. We must have looked like something out of 'The Beverly Hillbillies' – Episode Ten, in which the Clampetts hitch a lift with a hairdresser in his lime-green Beetle!

But eventually we arrived in Southern Spain – and the real journey began.

Chapter 3
Settling in

A month before we made our epic journey to Fuengirola, Chris had flown out to find a property we could rent for three weeks and use as a beach head while we sorted ourselves out a bit. We figured that three weeks would give us enough time to find a more permanent, unfurnished, property, so we'd paid through the nose for a town house at holiday-let prices. The house was in El Cotto, just outside Fuengirola, in what I would call the 'just okay' bracket, and Chris had only been able to view it from the outside, as it was allegedly occupied at the time of her visit. But, unfortunately, the niceness of the outside wasn't reflected on the inside. Don't get me wrong, it was clean, but the furniture was well past its sell-by date, and there was a permanent lavatorial smell on the ground floor that we never got to the bottom of – so to speak. We'd expected better, but it was too late and the agent already had our dosh, so we just chalked it up to experience and began looking for a more permanent rented home, guided by Chris's children Justine and Jonathan.

We didn't know the good areas from the bad, but we knew that we didn't want to live in the middle of town – and that we had just three weeks to find somewhere suitable, or we'd be moving into a hotel. One of the local English language newspapers comes out on a Friday and we worked our way through the property rental section and found a villa that sounded interesting, on the road up to the village of Mijas. So we phoned the agent for a viewing, and it was just what we were looking for: two bedrooms, two bathrooms, private gardens with palm trees and a private pool.

The property was furnished and, like the town house, the furniture was crap. So, through the agent, we asked the owner if he would take the furniture out, and he agreed. But the payback was that his furniture would have to go into our garage, which meant that my beloved Harley would only have a carport. It was a compromise I didn't like, but, as the villa was very nice, we went for it and signed an 11-month rental agreement at 1500 euros per month. Sorted!

They say that paying rent is a waste of money, but to Chris and me it was money well spent, because we know for an absolute fact that if we'd bought immediately, we'd have bought wrong. So we called in our own furniture from the removal company depot, together with my Harley, and settled into our new home. It didn't take us long to find our way around, and during the first few months we made various acquaintances – which was an experience in itself!

We had decided that we were going to take at least a year to look, listen and learn, but knew that ultimately we'd have to generate an income, as we didn't have enough capital to sit on our hands forever. Chris had always quite fancied having an English teashop. When returning from visiting her children, she'd often comment that there were hundreds of bars and restaurants in the area, but that she'd never seen anywhere you could sit and have a nice cup of English tea, served in a proper little ceramic teapot, and get a nicely presented sandwich.

So, after a few months of easing ourselves in to our new environment, we started to look around casually at potential sites for our teashop. What an eye opener that was! As a tourist, you can't look behind the scenes into the kitchen of bars and restaurants, but if you're looking with a view to buying, you obviously get the opportunity to see the lot. Never in my life did I even begin to imagine how absolutely filthy some of these places could be. If you can visualise a real dustbin student kitchen and double the filth, you still wouldn't be anywhere near imagining the squalor of some of these places. There were many occasions when we got to the kitchen door and turned on our heels without even going in. How do they get away with it? Christ knows. When we arrived at one bar in Torreblanca (East Fuengirola), the middle-aged couple who owned the lease were absolutely legless – at 11 o'clock in the morning. I kid you not, they were completely and utterly off their trolleys, which, we were to learn, is not particularly unusual.

Chris and I were in complete agreement about the fact that if we were to live and work in Spain, one thing was absolutely not negotiable: we had to be overlooking the sea. We didn't have any pre-conceived ideas on where to site our teashop, but highlighted two locations based on the volume of potential customers – Fuengirola and Benalmadena. Mijas Pueblo (*pueblo* = village) was a possibility at one stage, as the villa we were renting was close to Mijas and we loved the Spanish village atmosphere. But it wasn't long before we dismissed the idea due to the lack of tourists in winter and the absence of a sea view. You *can* see the sea from certain places in Mijas, but it's around three miles away!

At the same time as we were looking at potential businesses, we were also sussing out menus and pricing. Presumably because there are more bars and restaurants in Benalmadena, the prices there are generally cheaper, which was a negative as far as we were concerned: what's the point of working harder for longer hours for the same amount of money? So Fuengirola it had to be.

We looked at more bar and restaurant units than I care to remember and, to be honest, we got absolutely sick of it. So we decided to put the idea on the back burner and concentrate on our other potential business venture in advertising. The concept was quite simple: advertising on beer mats. It's big business in the UK and a number of people have made a lot of money out of it. Traditionally, beer mats were used to advertise beers, spirits and tobacco brands, but when tobacco advertising began to be frowned upon and was eventually banned, certain individuals began to ask themselves, 'Why not advertise other products on beer mats in pubs and restaurants?' The brand name is constantly in your face, spread all over tables wherever you go. A great idea!

As I've already mentioned, I'd been a director of a print group in the UK, and one of the companies printed beer mats. We hadn't been in Spain very long before I noticed that beer mats were rarely on display in bars, and when I asked a few bar owners about this, they told me that beer mats were hardly ever supplied by the Spanish brewers. If the beer representative did bring in mats, it would inevitably be one little pack of around 100, which many bars can go through in a single day.

Decision made. I had the contacts for the design and printing of the mats, and all I needed were the advertisers. So we formed an official SL company, which is the equivalent of a limited company in the UK, and bought one million mats from the UK to our own design, advertising the concept to potential advertisers in English on one side and Spanish on the other. We then proceeded to blanket bomb bars along the whole Costa del Sol with our mats, and I settled down next to the telephone to await the response, which I was confident would be almost immediate.

It wasn't. I learned the hard way that what is successful in the UK does not necessarily carry through over here. We did receive calls from local, relatively small, British-owned companies, but when I told them the price, they nearly fell off their chairs – they either couldn't afford it or weren't prepared to pay for it. I had meetings with various companies and in some cases the response was, 'I can't afford to pay all the money at once, but I'll pay some now and the balance later.' Now, I've been around the block a few times and it's bad enough being striped when you work for a company, but I imagine being striped for your own money is very painful. So no thanks.

I thought the major real-estate companies over here would jump at this new concept, but I was surprised and disappointed by their view that beer mats were 'not really in keeping with our image'. That's a laugh! What do they think their image is? Possibly they should do some market research on that one.

In the UK, most campaigns are generated and driven through advertising agencies. So Chris and I decided to hire an interpreter and spend some time in Seville, which is where the major ad agencies are for the area. We secured appointments with numerous agencies, but, again, disappointment was the order of the day. Drip mats are part of the UK culture: there aren't many pubs without beer mats advertising anything from airlines to recruitment agencies. But I quickly realised that the Spanish are not really tuned into the concept. When a meeting starts with the question 'What's a beer mat?', you know you're already on the back foot. I'd explain the concept through my interpreter and be met with puzzled expressions and comments such as, 'But when I put my glass on it, I cannot see the advertising.'

Never underestimate the difference in cultures!

It soon became apparent that the only way to kick this off was to try to generate business from UK companies that might be interested in advertising their brand or product to holidaymakers and ex-pats on the Costa del Sol. So I secured an order from The Sun newspaper 'News International', and the campaign went well: during the World Cup, every table in the many sports bars along the coast had mats advertising the newspaper in bold, bright red lettering. I was delighted, but my elation was short lived.

I spent an absolute fortune on telephone calls to the UK, speaking to literally hundreds of advertising managers, brand managers and marketing managers – and drew blank after blank. I still had contacts at large companies that own global and pan-European brands, and although some liked the idea, it was too niche for a major brand. One such company told me that if I could cover the whole of Spain, they'd be interested in pursuing it, but not for the Costa del Sol alone. There was no way I could even consider distributing beer mats throughout Spain – no resources! It was a complete non-starter. Just think of the logistics. Even if I were prepared to go for it, I'd be back to long hours and hassle, running round and round on the old hamster wheel again. No thanks.

What's key here is to remember that what works in the UK doesn't necessarily work in Spain – and often for reasons you wouldn't normally consider.

That initial experience in advertising cost Chris and me in the region of £20,000 – not a fortune to a company perhaps, but a painful experience to individuals (us).

Chapter 4

The Tea Tree

There are many free English language newspapers and magazines for Brits in Spain. I was reading the 'Businesses for sale' section in one of them just to pass the time one day when I noticed a small advertisement for a bar on the Paseo Maritimo (Promenade) in Fuengirola. We hadn't looked at any bars for a while, so we decided to phone the number and arrange to view it.

When we arrived we could hardly believe it: it was exactly what we were looking for – a coffee bar/café with a good-sized, clean, well-equipped kitchen, immaculately decorated throughout. You could walk in and start the next day. Perfect. To make things even better, although the lease wasn't cheap, the rent was a steal for the seafront (I'll explain the different lease costs and rents later), which was apparently because the occupiers prior to the people we bought it from had been running it as a kebab shop and had left it in one hell of a state. So the freehold owner had agreed to the low rent providing the new owners completely gutted the place and made something decent out of it. I have to say they'd done an excellent job, and we didn't need to think about it for long, as that kind of business, in that location, and at that level of rent, just didn't come up very often.

As the saying goes, 'He who dithers gets f*** all.' So we bought the lease, and once we'd signed the necessary papers and handed the money over, we were given the keys.

The one thing the unit didn't have was air conditioning. It was July and we'd seen the previous owners in action for a day just prior to taking the keys, and the sweat was literally dripping from the woman's nose while she was cooking. So the first thing I did was get a UK-owned air-conditioning company to install two large units, one in the bar area and one in the kitchen. In my opinion, this is the best money you'll spend if you decide to buy a café, bar or restaurant over here, particularly if you intend to cook.

Although the place was immaculate, there were things we needed to do in order to turn it into 'our teashop'. First of all we changed the name, as I think the name is absolutely paramount in putting over the right image and message: it has to tell people just what you do. Are you a coffee shop? A restaurant? A pub? We called ours The Tea Tree, which we felt had a nice ring to it.

The next job was to scour Malaga looking for individual ceramic teapots and little matching milk jugs, cups and saucers. We spoke to virtually every food and drinks supplier in the area to try to source the best goods at the right price, and we must have done a reasonable job, as, with only one exception, we retained the same suppliers throughout the time we had the café. The one supplier we decided to ditch was a guy who brought us a box of frozen Cajun Chicken pieces one day and we noticed the 'best before' date was four months earlier.

'Excuse me. This chicken is out of date.'

'Oh that's no problem. I eat it all the time and it doesn't do me any harm.'

'On your bike pal. You won't be supplying here any more.'

Stock rotation, quality control checks – none.

Next door to us was an evening bar and, as we had no intention of working evenings, we struck up an agreement with the owner. We would use his terrace during the day and he could use ours during the evening – a sort of timeshare terrace and a win/win agreement that doubled our outside capacity and worked well for both of us.

Chris and I didn't have a clue how many people it would take to run the business, but to avoid getting completely swamped we decided we'd take someone on to work on the terrace. As it happened, a girl had been in a few days previously asking for work and had left her telephone number, so we gave her a call. She explained that she had found a job but that she was over here for the summer season with her best friend, Emma, who was still looking. Fine. We arranged to meet Emma, and she was a terrific girl. So that was that; sorted. Let's get cracking.

We were utterly clueless. Emma had no terrace experience, as she'd worked for a building society on the Isle of Man, and Chris and I didn't have a clue either. It was mid-August and the first few days were horrific, as we hadn't anticipated how busy we'd be. We'd already dramatically changed the menu, because the previous owner's menu was far too complicated. Keep it simple. Most of our business, apart from the obvious teas and coffees, was toasted sandwiches and freshly filled baguettes. Although we didn't want to do breakfasts, we realised we had to, as 'the English breakfast' is what many, if not most, Brits want in the morning when they're on holiday. The original inherited menu had three breakfast choices: a small breakfast, a standard breakfast, and what was called a 'mega breakfast', which was a full heart attack on a plate. To hell with that; we did the standard breakfast and that was it.

You would not believe the trouble a breakfast can cause. To be fair, I don't suppose most people have any idea about the cost-and-profit margins involved in running a café, but you always get some who try it on and want something for nothing. The sausages and bacon are by far the most expensive components of a breakfast, but we would regularly get people saying:

'I don't like tomatoes; can I have an extra sausage instead?' *No.*

'The breakfast comes with two eggs. I only want one egg. Can I have an extra piece of bacon instead?' *No.*

To begin with, our breakfast price included a tea or coffee, and we'd get couples in saying words to the effect of:

'One breakfast please. My wife doesn't want anything as she'll have the free tea I get with my breakfast'. *Oh, that's all right then.*

So, within a couple of weeks, the menus were changed again, with the tea and coffee charged separately. But we still hadn't completely solved the problem. The breakfast came with a small complimentary orange juice:

'Instead of the orange juice, could I have a coffee?' *No.*

One couple came in and the man asked for a breakfast. Fine. The woman then said:

'You see this two slices of toast with jam and butter? Could I swap the jam portion for bacon?' *No.*

How the hell can you compare a small jam portion with bacon?

We even had one cheeky so-and-so who asked if he could swap the complimentary orange juice for a strawberry milkshake. It wouldn't be so bad if they had a wry smile on their faces when they asked, but in most cases they look at you as if you're being completely unreasonable when you refuse.

There's another strange thing that I never really got to the bottom of. If you were asking for two breakfasts, what would you say?

Personally, I would say, 'Two breakfasts please.' But I reckon nearly 50 per cent of our customers said, 'Two breakfastses please.' So if you ask for six breakfasts, should you say 'Six breakfastseseseseses please'?

We pressed on through the first few weeks and Emma turned out to be an absolute brick. She was brilliant with the customers, and although she only worked part time (10.00 a.m.–2.00 p.m.), she'd be there within minutes of us phoning her if we got battered. She stayed on the terrace taking orders and clearing the tables, and Chris and I alternated in the kitchen, with one of us in the middle doing the drinks and the till. When things got stressful, which was almost all the time at the beginning, an order would be ready in the kitchen and Emma would be chatting to a customer or taking an order on the terrace when a deafening shout of 'Emmaaaaaaaaa' would suddenly echo through the building, and the poor girl would colour up and fly in to collect the order.

Chris and I would feel terrible when we shouted at Emma, but she just got on with doing a superb job. I apologised to her one day and tried to explain that it was all new to us and that we were getting stressed out, and she just turned round in her kind, mild manner and said, 'It's okay Stuart. I understand. You can bollock me if you want. I don't mind.' We felt dreadful, and never shouted again.

Unfortunately, after Emma had been working for us for about seven months, her friend decided she wanted to go back home, and one person on bar wages couldn't generate enough money to pay for an apartment and all the living costs. So, reluctantly, Emma went back too, but we still keep in touch with her and remain friends. She was a great girl, and during the relatively short time we knew her, she became like a daughter to us.

In our previous working lives, Chris and I had never worked directly with the public, and in some respects opening the teashop was one hell of a shock. We'd already decided to open for only six or seven hours a day, and settled on 9.30 a.m. to 3.30 p.m. Many of the bar owners over here open at 10.00 a.m. (ish) and then don't finish until daft o'clock the next morning. No thank you. During the winter months we worked six days a week, closing on Sundays, but during the busy summer months we closed an extra day a week, on Saturdays. Now this seemed logical to us, but it really confused other people, particularly other bar and restaurant owners, as their aim was to work as many hours as humanly possible during the summer in order to make hay while the sun shone. But that wasn't for us; if we hit the number of customers we required in order to cover all our costs, then that was it. In the summer, we could do that and more in five days, so we closed the extra day. If we went through a period of taking a battering every day, we'd sometimes have a spur-of-the-moment day off, which we called a 'St F***-It Day', and I have to say that he is, by far, my favourite patron saint.

During the whole time we had our business, I really couldn't say which days were the busiest. The only predictable thing about owning a bar or café is the unpredictability. One week we'd be bombed out on a Tuesday and quiet on the Friday. The following week it could be exactly the opposite. And the same applied to mornings and afternoons. There was no pattern whatsoever, which usually made it impossible to plan to bring in extra staff at certain times or on specific days.

We were fortunate in that we didn't need to generate much money, and we were determined to enjoy our new life rather than swap the old hamster wheel for a new one in the sun. We hadn't come to Spain to get rich; it was the lifestyle that attracted us. So if we could cover all our costs for both the business and home, we'd be happy. It was hard work during the summer months, but we were looking at the sea all day, which was wonderful. I often thought to myself, 'This is great. I used to make decisions about buying £1,000,000+ printing presses, and now all I worry about is if we're going to run out of lettuce.'

There were many times during the winter months when we were very quiet for an hour or more. If it was a nice day, Chris would often take a little chair over to the beach and read her book in the sun. She'd keep looking over to see if any customers came in and, if they did, would be back in less than a minute. Perfect. What more could you want?

Many an idle hour was spent watching the *grúa* truck, which is basically what you and I would call a breakdown truck. In Spain, if a car is illegally parked, the *grúa* truck will appear and tow it away. They take no prisoners. If you park in the wrong place, your car will be gone when you return – and what a performance to get it back. You have to go to the police station to pay a fine and then to the vehicle compound to pay another amount of money, which can equate to around £120.

All along the seafront in Fuengirola are pay and display parking bays. As it happened, the bay directly outside our teashop was for loading and unloading only, i.e. Coca Cola, San Miguel deliveries etc. There was actually a parking ticket machine there, which was naughty, because it understandably made many people assume that it was a legitimate pay and display parking area. There was also a sign informing people of the fact that it was for loading and unloading only, but this was placed directly behind a tree trunk so you couldn't see it.

It is a cast-iron fact that the *grúa* truck, often directed by one or two policemen, would always tow away the hire cars and foreign-plated cars first. The Spanish-plated cars were almost always left, at least until last, if not permanently. It's not fair, but it's a fact. Resident Brits would sometimes sit on our terrace and take bets on which car would be the first to go. It was easy money, because if there was a hire car there (you could spot these, as they were inevitably fairly new with no wheel trims) or a foreign-plated car, it would go first. You could bank on it.

Talking about *grúa* trucks reminds me that we had our car towed away once. I parked in what I thought was a legitimate parking place, as there were no yellow lines in sight, but what I hadn't noticed were the large wheelie bins on the pavement nearby. When Chris and I came back, the car was gone, and there was only one explanation: the *grúa* truck. Of course, it could have been stolen, but that seemed highly unlikely, bearing in mind its colour.

I went round to the local police station and told them that I thought our car had been towed away, and we had the following conversation – in Spanish, which left me at somewhat of a disadvantage, as my Spanish wasn't very good.

'What kind of car is it?' asked the policeman behind the desk.

'Er, er.' I didn't know what the word for beetle was in Spanish. 'It's um, well; it's er…'

'What kind of car is it?' he asked again, a little less sympathetically.

I did know what the word for cockroach was, so I just went with that. 'Cucaracha,' I said firmly.

The policeman glanced down involuntarily at the floor and then turned to look behind him. Relieved at seeing no cockroaches, and obviously starting to get a bit annoyed, he asked again.

'What kind of car is it?'

'It's a cucaracha – a Volkswagen cucaracha'.

Suddenly the penny seemed to drop. 'Ah, si. What colour is it?'

Oh hell, this was going to be difficult. You may have seen a new-shaped Volkswagen Beetle in the same colour as ours. You'll certainly remember if you have, because it's the most stupid colour you've ever seen in your life. I think its official name is actually 'lime yellow', which just about sums it up: it's not green and it's not yellow; it's somewhere in the middle. But I had no idea what 'lime yellow' was in Spanish.

'It's not green and it's not yellow,' I said, helpfully.

'Well what colour is it then?' the policeman asked, speaking slowly and clearly.

'It's sort of green and sort of yellow.'

It was obvious that his patience was wearing thin. 'So, is it green or is it yellow?'

I decided it was time to make a decision. 'Er, er – yellow,' I said.

'Okay, yellow. Now, what is the registration number?'

We still had our British registration at the time and the letters were AJO – which means 'garlic' in Spanish. Whenever we stopped at a zebra crossing or traffic lights, people would stare in amazement at the colour – which isn't available in Spain – and then start laughing when they noticed the number plate. Nervously, I spelled it out.

The policeman stood up and leaned towards me across the counter, and for a fleeing moment the thought crossed my mind that he was going to nut me on the forehead. But with his face about an inch from mine, he just glared at me and then sat back down and repeated his question.

'What's the registration number?'

I told him again, and I think it crossed his mind to arrest me for taking the piss, or else to breathalyse me, but, thankfully, he obviously decided to give me the benefit of the doubt.

We got the car back, although in some respects it might have been good if it *had* been stolen, so that we'd have been able to replace it with a white car with registration letters that meant nothing in any language.

Another pastime of ours when we were quiet was to watch the local alcis – Spain has its fair share – who congregated across the road on the beach. What a great set of guys! In the UK they'd probably be abusive, but for some reason that's not the case over here. In fact, probably the only thing these guys did have in common with their British counterparts was that they too had dogs that they led around at the end of lengths of string.

They'd start to arrive at the same spot around 9.30 a.m. with their plastic bags full of Cruz Campo beer cans and proceed to have their breakfast. Once the breakfast bag ran out, there'd be a constant procession from the beach to the local bakery for more cans. (Yes, the bakery sells beer – this country just sounds better and better, doesn't it lads!) As the day went on, the laughter would increase until, around midday, they'd just go into a coma. Another good day over.

29

Although these guys were off their heads most of the time, they were very friendly and we got to know some of them quite well. If we had a problem, they'd always help us out, borrow a euro, which you'd never see again, and then fall over, before starting the whole routine again the next day.

So, to conclude, what's the one unequivocal thing that can be said about running a café or bar in Spain? There's never a dull moment.

Chapter 5
The good, the bad – and the delusional

Chris and I have met some really tremendous people in Spain, as well as a number of completely useless twonkers. The Costas are a magnet for the British, and there are some great Brits living here, but never before have I come across such a tight concentration of gold-plated idiots. You could make a hobby out of sitting in British bars just listening to the absolute twaddle coming out of some people's mouths and wondering if it's 'National Talking Bollocks Day'. I'm not talking about tourists, but about Brits who actually live here.

For example, you have the 'yeah right millionaire' who looks (and is) anything but a millionaire. Don't get me wrong, there are lots of genuine British millionaires on the Costas – as witnessed by some of the houses – but there are also lots of two-penny millionaires who sit in pubs, hammered, and spout forth complete twaddle about how rich they are. Then there are the cowboy builders who sit there at 2 o'clock in the afternoon telling you how busy they are – which is, of course, why they can afford the time to be smashed and in the bar at 2 in the afternoon.

Many of the Brits living in the major resorts on the Costas are hiding from something, or someone – the tax man, the police, the bank, a credit company, the Child Support Agency, or, in a few cases, all of the above. We've met and heard of numerous people who cannot or dare not go back to the UK for various reasons.

Due to the ease of obtaining credit in the UK, it's not unusual for Brits to build up the confidence of a bank, take out a loan for £10,000, £20,000, or more, and then jump the country for a new life in Spain. Others run up huge debts on credit cards, go to the limit and then leg it to the nearest airport, arrive in Spain and proceed to get everything wrong and burn all the money in a relatively short period of time. Because of the difficulties of finding a 'proper' job (which I'll go into in more detail later), they are then seriously up shit creek without a paddle. They can't afford to live in Spain and yet they dare not go back to criminal charges in the UK.

We became acquainted with one woman who had done just that – taken out a loan and then come to Spain and spent it all. Fortunately for her, she had a son in the UK who'd made a reasonable amount of money in a business. So, as a last resort, she asked him for financial help and, being the loving son he was, he agreed to lend (give) her £10,000. Unfortunately for her, presumably due to the fact that her son wasn't aware that his mother had done a runner with a bank loan, he transferred the money straight into her UK account. The bank in question was the same one that had given her the loan, and – surprise, surprise – said 'Thank you very much,' and kept the ten grand. Believe it or not, this lady was spitting blood all around Fuengirola, saying how unfair it was that the bank had kept *her* money. She sincerely believed they had acted unjustly and that the money was hers by right. Needless to say, the last thing she wanted was for the bank to know her whereabouts, so that was that. Thanks a lot son, back to trying to find a job in a bar I guess.

Any of you who have ever worked in a shop, pub, restaurant or with the public in general will know what I mean when I say that Chris and I were simply not prepared for some of the things that happened, or for some of the daft comments that were made to us whilst in The Tea Tree. You have to put up with all kinds of things. Sometimes you take an instant dislike to people before they've even opened their mouths, and although occasionally you find they're actually very nice people, more often than not you are spot on. To give you a flavour of some of these, I've listed a few examples below.

'Do you live here?'

No we commute from Leeds/Bradford Airport every morning. What do you think?

'Do you sell monkey tea?'

'Pardon.'

'You know, monkey tea. Do you sell it?'

'I'm sorry; I don't know what you're talking about.'

'Monkey tea. I can't remember its proper name. Monkey tea, do you sell it?'

The penny dropped: she meant PG Tips.

'Will it be hot tomorrow?'

*How the f*** do I know?*

'A coffee please.'

'Certainly. Black or white?'

'Brown please.'

Eh?

'Do you speak English?'

Me, thinking I'm having a laugh: 'Well Yorkshire; it's similar.'

'Oh that's a shame. I really wanted someone who speaks English.'

Hmm. Perhaps you should be concentrating more on what it is you <u>need</u>.

'A scone with cream and jam please. How many servings do you get in a scone?'

Am I really supposed to answer that one?

'I think I would like toast and marmalade. Could I have a look at a piece of your toast please?'

What?

'A BLT please, but with no bacon, tomato or mayo.'

So that's just a lettuce sandwich then.

For the next one you need to imagine a slack-looking girl with a very strong south Yorkshire accent.

'Av yer got spo-i-dick?' (*She meant spotted dick, which in the north of England is a pudding.*)

'No sorry. We have apple pie, scones, cheesecake and chocolate fudge cake.'

'Aw, I wan-ed spo-i-dick really. Aven't ya got any spo-i-dick?'

'No sorry.'

'Aw – amt yer got any spo-i-dick at all?'

No, no, no.

One day a rather large lady came in with an older couple, who I think were her parents.

Older lady: 'A prawn salad baguette please.'

Man: 'A tuna salad baguette please.'

Large lady: 'A prawn salad baguette please, if they're big. Oh, and a cheese and ham toasty, and I think I'll have cheesecake and cream please. I don't know why I'm ordering so much; it must be my nerves.'

Yes, that's what it must be, your nerves.

People also often used to ask us questions when they had no intention whatsoever of taking any notice of our answers, and sometimes they even seemed to hold us responsible for answers they didn't like. The following are just a couple of examples.

'Can you drink the tap water here?'

'Yes. The water is extremely good quality here.'

'Wouldn't you go to the expense of buying bottled water then?'

'No. It's perfectly okay to use the tap water for either boiling in the kettle or even for drinking straight out of a glass.'

'Oh, are you sure that it's okay?'

'Yes. It's very good.'

'No. I daren't. I think we'll carry on buying the bottled water'.

Why the hell bother asking me then?

'Do you know how much they charge for the paragliding on the beach?'

'Yes. It's thirty euros and it normally lasts about ten minutes.'

'Oh, that's expensive.'

'Err, well, that's about the going rate wherever you go.'

'Thirty euros! That's a bit steep.'

'Yes, well, that's how much it is.'

'I'm not paying that! I don't know how they get away with it. That's daylight robbery. How on earth can they justify that?'

You asked me how much it was and I told you. I don't own the bloody paragliding thingy and I certainly don't fix the prices. Why pick on me?

I hate televisions in pubs or cafés unless it's a sports bar where you know that there will be a TV in order to watch the football, horse racing or whatever it is that you want to watch. The Tea Tree didn't have a TV (over my dead body) and, generally speaking, the people who came in didn't want to sit gawping at some trashy programme whilst having their tea and scones. However, a couple came in once, sat down on the terrace and ordered a drink and a sandwich each, and all's perfectly fine. Then I noticed that the guy's head was shooting round in all directions as if he was looking for something or somebody. I didn't think much about it, and went out onto the terrace to take an order from the next table. As I was walking past, this guy stopped me.

'You haven't got a TV.'

How bloody observant. 'No, that's right. We don't have a TV.'

'Why not?'

'Pardon?'

'Why haven't you got a TV?'

'Because I don't want one.'

'Yes, but we want to watch whateveritwas and you haven't got a TV.'

'Oh, right. You want to watch the TV and we haven't got one. What should I do? I could nip out and buy one, or go to another bar and borrow one. Or, erm, I know. I've just had a great idea!'

'What?'

'I could do absolutely nothing, which is exactly what I am going to do.'

'There's no need to be like that.'

'Like what? I've told you that we haven't got a bloody telly.

Is it me? Is it? Please tell me. Am I unreasonable?

Another thing you don't consider when you decide to move into this kind of business is that you have to be all things to all men – waiter, cook, cleaner, provider of tourist information, agony aunt, weather forecaster, entertainer – which isn't easy when you're busy. And, added to all that, I occasionally also inadvertently did stints as 'Sales Prevention Officer' – but more of that later.

Then there are the stereotypes.

The bar-front bore. When we first opened, we put stools for people to sit on at the front of the bar. Big mistake. There's nothing worse than being busy and having some dollop in front of you talking about things in which you have no interest whatsoever. You look up and there he is – 'Bell-end Billy the Bar-front Bore'. It's not a pub and I certainly ain't no landlord. Is there an art to being boring? It seems to me that some people can talk for 10 or 15 minutes and yet say absolutely nothing. Some don't even talk; they drone. Others try to tell you jokes and are about as funny as a dead bat. It only took three days before the bar stools went into a skip.

The terrace hoggers. There are some people who just want a free sun bed. They'd come in, usually in pairs, order the cheapest drinks on the menu and then get out their books. They'd always sit at a table that was directly in the sun and, if possible, at the front of the terrace with the best view of the sea, and after ten minutes would have taken one sip from their drinks. They'd continually shuffle their chairs around to follow the sun, and you could tell they intended staying there for the day. It wasn't a problem if things were quiet, but if we were busy and they could see they were taking up a table for four unnecessarily, wouldn't you think they'd have the decency to drink up and clock off?

Sometimes my patience would run out and I'd be out there. 'Excuse me, but, as you can see, we're full and people are walking past because there are no seats. Will you be long?' In some cases they'd look slightly embarrassed, pay their bill and away they'd go. There are, however, the 'I know my rights' merchants:

'I am paying for this drink and will take as long as I like over it.'

'No, you are not paying for it, as I am taking it off you. Let's just say that the drink was free. Goodbye.'

Who needs their two euros?

The tightwads. We had a sign outside, advertising take-away baguettes for the beach or airport. People would come in for a take-away, look at the menu on the bar, and say things like:

'Is there a reduction in these prices if I don't eat in?'

No. We charge more, as you're getting it wrapped in tin foil and a plastic carrier bag. Just piss off.

'I see you get salad garnish with the baguettes. As I'm taking it away, could I have chips instead of the salad garnish'?

No. You can piss off as well.

One danger sign is the person who comes in, looks at the menu, and then asks for something completely and utterly different from anything on it. We had lots of them. It was a teashop, a café, call it what you want, but it certainly wasn't either an à la carte restaurant or a pick and mix shop.

One example was a guy who came in and wanted two eggs well done, but not too well done – he thinks he's buying a steak – two slices of bacon and two slices of toast. I could tell immediately he was a complainer. Now I am not a chef, but I can understand it when cooks and chefs tell me that one person like that with a non-standard order when you're busy can cock up the flow of things completely in a kitchen.

At that time, our breakfast was priced on the menu at 4 euros 90 cents and consisted of two eggs, two rashers of bacon, one sausage, beans, tomatoes and a slice of toast. As Chris, quite understandably, saw this as an oddball order, we wrote out the bill at 5 euros and 15 cents. Sure enough, we watched him look at the bill, pick up the menu, and then call one of us over. I was ready for him.

'I have had two eggs, two slices of bacon and two slices of toast, and yet you have charged me more than a full breakfast, which includes a sausage, beans, tomatoes and an orange juice.'

'That's right, *but* there are two ways of looking at this. As you will also see on the menu, two scrambled eggs on toast cost 3 euros 75 cents; if you then add the two slices of bacon at 70 cents each, you can see where we get the price from.'

'But that's not the way *I* am looking at it. I know about these things; my father was a waiter many years ago.'

I swear I just flipped. The guy was arguing about pennies and I don't need it.

'I don't give two tin shits if your father was the Prime Minister. Just leave what you want to pay and I suggest you go somewhere else in the future. I don't need your money.'

Calm down Stuart!

There was also a German couple – well, they might have been Austrian; I'm quite good with accents, so it was definitely one or the other. They were probably mid-sixties; they sat down at the front of our terrace in the sun, in the best seats in the house, and I went out to take their order.

'Hello, what can I get for you?'

The lady said, 'Get me a cappuccino.'

I let those bad manners go, as I like to think I make allowances for differences in culture, and turned to the guy.

'Nothing. I don't want anything.'

Okay, so that's one cappuccino on a table for four at the front of the terrace in the sun. I must have been in a good mood because I just went inside and got the lady a cappuccino, which I placed in front of her.

I was halfway back across the terrace when I heard, 'Get me a plate.' Eh? Is she talking to me? Now I'm getting seriously annoyed.

'Why?' I said.

'Because I don't want all this creamy froth on the top.'

'Why not order an ordinary coffee then?' I said.

Bite your tongue Stuart. I went back in and brought the 'lady' a saucer and then had to bite my tongue again as I watched her scoop the froth onto it.

I looked outside a couple of minutes later and she'd got a plastic bag from somewhere and had begun eating her own sandwiches out of it.

That was it. I legged it out hell bent on one ambition: to kick these people out.

'Excuse me. You can't eat your own food in here.'

'What?' said the husband.

'You heard me. You can't eat your own food in here.'

'Have you ever been to France?' he said.

'Well, actually, yes; I worked there for a while.'

'Well, it's quite normal to do this in France'.

Now think this through: you have a German/possibly Austrian, talking to an Englishman, in Spain, about France – *what's that got to do with the price of fish?*

I picked up the coffee cup, minus the froth, and told them to get the hell out.

On another day, a late-middle-aged couple came in accompanied by two guys who appeared to be in their twenties. As it happened, I wasn't working that day, for reasons I can't remember, so we had a friend working in the kitchen and Chris was covering the terrace. She went over to these people to take their order, and the elderly couple both asked for a breakfast.

Then one of the younger guys said, 'I'll have a breakfast as well, but I only want egg whites.'

'I beg your pardon,' said Chris.

'Egg whites,' he repeated irritably. 'I only want egg whites. It's not so difficult is it?'

Chris says she was only seconds away from whacking the arrogant prat over the head with her tray.

'Look,' the guy said slowly, as though talking to an imbecile. 'It's quite easy. You just get two cups, crack the eggs into one of the cups, pour the whites into the other cup, and then fry the whites only. You can understand that, can't you?'

Now, Chris is a very nice, pleasant, considerate person, who'll happily help people when she can – but... don't mess with her, and don't push her beyond the line.

'I do understand,' she said. 'I understand perfectly. Egg whites only.'

'That's right,' the guy replied, as though he was congratulating a small child. 'I'm glad we've sorted that out.'

'Not quite,' said Chris quietly.

'What do mean, "Not quite"?' the guy asked.

'What I mean is that you think I'm a waitress and that you can talk to me like a piece of shit, when in fact I own this place. I could buy and sell you fifteen times over. So you can take your attitude, together with your friends, and piss off.'

That's not like Chris, and I might have thought she was exaggerating a bit if our friend hadn't happened to come out of the kitchen and hear it – she still talks about it to this day.

The older guy hung back and apologised to Chris, but I don't think she was really listening.

One day, a couple came in with a young child who looked about four years old. I walked out to take their order and they were very pleasant, and obviously Scandinavian. They ordered a couple of coffees and toasted sandwiches and said that the child, who was eating an ice lolly, wouldn't require anything. Okay, no problem.

I went into the bar, pinned the food order in the kitchen and then made the two coffees, put them on a tray, together with the relevant cutlery, condiments and serviettes, walked back out towards the sun terrace, and nearly dropped the whole lot. I thought I must be seeing things. The lady was casually leaning back on her chair with her bikini top pulled down and this four-year-old child locked onto one of her boobs, still with ice lolly in hand. I didn't know what to do, but, being British after all, I put everything down on their table and pretended nothing was happening – and then legged it into the kitchen and told Chris what was going on.

'He can't be four years old,' she said. 'Don't be ridiculous. You know what you men are like: you don't know the difference between a four-year-old child and an 18-month-old toddler.'

'Okay, you go out then.' I said. 'I'm not exaggerating, honest.'

Chris laughed, and went out onto the terrace and pretended to be messing about with something on another table, before returning, open mouthed.

'You're right!' she gasped. 'He's definitely at least four. He keeps stopping to take a lick of his ice lolly. That's disgusting! It's not right. You need to go out and say something to them.'

But, of course, neither of us said anything. What the hell *could* you say?

People who don't take sugar. It happened literally hundreds of times: I'd take a cup of coffee or tea out to a table with the standard-issue spoon and paper tube of sugar on the saucer. The 'non-sugar taker' would then proceed to lift the paper sugar tube by the corner to eye level, pulling a pained face as though it was radioactive, and say, 'You can take this back. I don't take sugar.' So f***ing what. Why can't they just leave it on the saucer until they've finished their drink? It's as though they think that not taking sugar is some kind of highly admirable virtue and they want the whole world to know.

The Brit who's learnt a bit of Spanish. The Tea Tree was a typically English name, and we had a full-size Union Jack flying outside. The customers are obviously English, and I've asked them, in English, what they'd like.
'Dos café con leche por favor.'
So that's two coffees with milk then.

The cosmopolitan jet-set Spaniards. These guys would come in occasionally, usually if there were a couple of good-looking British girls on the terrace, and sit there laughing and generally trying to impress the ladies. We had a couple of flash boys in once and sure enough they sat next to a couple of blonde girls on our terrace. I walked up to them and asked what they'd like.
'Two Martinis on the rocks, but with no ice please.'
You cocked that one up lads.

The 'instant-service' people. Wouldn't you think that when people are on holiday they'd be relaxed? Not always. We had a woman who came in once with her son, who I guess was about five years old. They sat down and, for whatever reason, she was obviously not in a very good mood. As usual, I gave her a couple of minutes and then went out to take her order, but she wafted me away rudely and told me she wasn't ready yet.

As it happened, two couples came in together at that point and one of the men said to me 'We are starving. Four breakfasts please.' I took the order straight to the kitchen and then went back out to the woman, whose son was creating holy hell, screaming and throwing things around. She was still quite rude, and asked for a proper mix and match mish-mash of things. Fair enough. I took her order into the kitchen.

A short while later, the four breakfasts were ready, so I took them out to the two couples and, as I was walking past this woman, she said to me, '**Excuse me**! I was here before these people and I haven't had my food yet.'

No problem, madam. I picked up her coffee cup together with Damian's coke glass and said, 'If you want instant service, there's a McDonalds down the road and I suggest you go there.' I then shouted through to the kitchen, 'Chris, cancel that order. The lady's leaving.'

You don't have to put up with that crap from anyone. Who do they think they are?

People with accents. It's very easy to misunderstand someone from another European country, even though they speak perfect English. One day, a Dutch lady walked onto our terrace and asked me for a coffee and a cheese and ham toasty. A short while later, when she'd eaten her sandwich, her husband arrived. I was doing something at the time, so Chris went out to take his order. When she returned, she was mumbling something to herself and looked annoyed, so I asked her what was wrong.

'What a tosser!' she said. 'Some Brits come over here and think they can get absolutely everything they can get in the UK. We're in Spain for Christ's sake. He asked me for toast with lemon cheese. Where in Spain can you get lemon cheese? I've told him we only have toast and marmalade.'

A moment later, the gentleman in question walked in looking confused and said to me, in a Dutch accent, 'Why can't I have toast with ham and cheese? You must have it, as my wife has just eaten it.'

It must have been the accent that made it sound to Chris like 'lemon cheese'.

People with a flaming cheek. There was one fairly elderly couple who rented an apartment in the block above our teashop. They came over for a month, two or three times a year, but hardly ever came into our place, except for the odd coffee and to borrow things. In fact, they borrowed a vase once and kept it for a month. I can't put my finger on the reason why, but this woman really irritated me.

When they arrived for one of their holidays, she came in and told me that her Uncle Fred was very ill in England and, as they didn't have a telephone in their apartment, she'd given her daughter our telephone number in case something happened. A bit cheeky I thought, but what could I do. For the next ten days or so this woman came in religiously two or three times a day to ask if there were any messages. It began to really piss me off, as they never bought anything. What is this, a bloody messaging service?

One day, the phone rang when we were very busy and when I answered it the daughter explained who she was. She went to great lengths to tell me that her parents were very good customers of ours, and asked if I could give her mother a message. I told her that her parents hardly, if ever, came in to our place except to ask if there were any messages. Anyway, the message was that 'Unfortunately, Uncle Fred has passed away.'

We were still very busy an hour or so later and were running round the terrace like lunatics when I saw this lady walking past. I must have been in a foul mood (again) and I am not proud of this, but I just lost it and ran to the front of the terrace and shouted, 'Excuse me, it's your Uncle Fred.' 'Yes?' she said. 'He's dead' – oh shit, did I really say that? Off to hide in the kitchen again.

The lavatory users. Allegedly, by Spanish law you cannot refuse anyone a glass of water or the use of the toilets. But after only a couple of weeks of both Spaniards and tourists coming in to use the loo, we had to take action. As it happened, there was construction work going on near us for well over a year, which we realised gave us a perfect excuse. Chris or I would say, 'I'm ever so sorry, but the construction workers have cut through the water supply and it won't be back on for approximately an hour.' Now, our Spanish wasn't very good, so explaining this to the Spaniards was more difficult: 'Lo siento, construction aqui corto agua,' accompanied by furious gesticulating, as it only half made sense to a Spaniard. We must have looked demented, but at least it worked – well, would you want to go to the loo in a café run by someone who was quite obviously crazy?

Dirty table hunters. Why is it that you can have a café/bar full of perfectly clean tables except one which has just been vacated, and someone will walk in and sit at that one solitary dirty table? What's wrong with them? It happened to us lots of times and I used to think they were having a laugh or taking the mickey. Come on; think about it. If you walked into a café which was virtually empty and saw a table which had not yet been cleared and loads of others which had; which table would you choose?

They're not right in their heads are they?

Book robbers. Chris and I read a lot of books and customers would often leave us books they had purchased at the airport and finished. As such, we had a table in The Tea Tree full of books with a little note offering people the opportunity to swap a book which a future customer might find to be of interest with one of ours. It's a fact of life, unfortunately, that there are always a few people who will take advantage and sometimes a person would try to walk out with a handful of books and not even leave one book in return. That's great isn't it – spend one euro fifty on a cup of coffee and walk off with twenty quids worth of books. I'm after them –

'Excuse me but why are you walking away with six books without even asking'.

'They're free aren't they?'

'Well yes they are, but the idea is that you leave your finished book and take away another one in return'.

'Oh, I thought they were free and I could just help myself'.

'Yea right, you either have a very large family with you or you're one hell of a speed reader'.

Amongst these books we had a Spanish/English dictionary in order for tourists to look up   whatever word or translation they required. Someone even nicked that!

What are these people on? Are they being serious?

Sometimes you get it completely wrong. One afternoon, a couple came in. The woman looked a bit butch and much younger than the guy, but it was only when I got to the table to take their order that I realised that the guy wasn't a guy at all. They ordered their food and a couple of drinks and everything was fine.

As it happened, we were very quiet at the time; in fact, they were the only people in. After a few minutes, I noticed that Chris was talking to these two people, and as I wandered out onto the terrace to join them, she said to me, 'This man wants to know where the best place to change money is.' Oh shit.

'Chris,' I tried to whisper, 'shut up please.'

'What? He just wants to know where to go to get some money changed.'

'Err, Chris, sorry to be rude, but there's a problem in the kitchen. Please come. It won't take a minute.'

'Yes, but this man has paid and is going now. He wants to change some money.'

I legged it to the kitchen, put my hands over my eyes and crouched on the floor. I don't know who I thought I was hiding from, but when Chris came in, quite annoyed, she looked thoroughly confused, and asked me, reasonably enough, 'What the hell are you playing at? You embarrassed me out there.'

'I embarrassed you! For Christ's sake, that bloke's a woman.'

'What bloke's a woman? What are you on about? That man wants some help with directions, that's all.'

'That's the point love. That man isn't a man; he's a woman.'

'He can't be… Oh hell. I daren't go back out there now. Are you sure she isn't a man?'

Fortunately, the two ladies had done everyone a favour and left, otherwise we'd both have had to stay in the kitchen all day.

Tipping. If you go into a place and are happy with the food that's served to you and with the level of attention and service you receive, then it's normal to leave a tip. It's not obligatory, but I think it's fair to say that most of us do it, particularly when abroad on our holidays. There's certainly no need for it if someone just has a drink, but if they have a meal and feel as though they've been made welcome, then yes, X euros, ten per cent of the bill value, whatever. The one thing that really pissed me off was when someone left 5 cents, or even just 1 cent. I take that as a complete insult and would much prefer they just said 'Thanks,' walked out and left nothing.

One day, a Scandinavian couple came in to our teashop, had a couple of drinks and something to eat and then asked for their bill, all very pleasant. They also commented on how nice the food had been. I took the bill to their table, they paid, and then they sat there for a couple of minutes before starting to walk away. I then took an empty tray out to clear the table and found three 1-cent coins on it. About two pence, thanks a bunch. I must have been in a bad mood I guess, as I just picked up the three coins and chucked them along the pavement after this couple, who looked round in astonishment, and then the lady proceeded to pick up all three of the tiny coins and put them in her pocket.

Thieves. People will steal almost anything that isn't nailed or screwed down. Shortly after we first opened the teashop, a Moroccan-looking guy came in one day for a glass of tap water. Next to the draught beer tap on the bar we had a small basket where we kept the tips, and customers would often throw a euro or whatever into it. Chris was in the kitchen, and I turned my back for what must have been just a few seconds to fill a glass with water and then handed it to him. He took only a small sip and then left, which I thought was strange, but then, about ten minutes later, I noticed the tip basket had gone. The bastard! I gave him a glass of water and he nicked our tips. It's not easy lifting a basket full of loose coins without making any noise whatsoever. Chris was seriously miffed and kept going on and on about it. It was probably only 10 or 15 euros, but that wasn't the point: we'd earned it and he'd nicked it.

Then, a few days later, the ice man came in. For convenience, bars buy ice cubes in bags, and on this particular day the normal ice man must have been ill or something, as it was a different guy. Now, to picture this properly, you need to understand that 'ice' in Spanish is 'hielo', pronounced 'yellow', and instead of pronouncing 'euro' as we do, the Spanish say 'aero'. Okay, this different ice man came to the door and shouted to us, 'Hielo?' Chris's reaction took me completely by surprise, and wasn't at all like her. She started jumping up and down with steam coming out of her ears, shouting at me, 'I'm sick of this. Tell him to piss off. He's begging. He's asking for a euro. He looks like that guy who stole our tips.'

'Calm down,' I said. 'It's the ice man. He said hielo – you know, ice.'

'Oh, that's all right then. Are you sure it's not him?'

The poor guy looked very sheepish every time he came in afterwards until the normal ice man returned.

You would not believe the things people will steal while on holiday. We regularly lost toilet rolls, air fresheners from the toilets, serviettes, and someone once stole a teapot lid – why not the whole pot for Christ's sake?

Sometimes people would ask for extra sugar or butter portions and Chris and I would watch them out of the corner of our eye. It used to have us in stitches. When they thought nobody was looking, they'd pick up the sugar sachets and slide them into their pocket or bag. On a couple of occasions, just out of devilment, I shouted out, 'Oi, I saw you nicking that sugar,' and then watched them colour up and look around in acute embarrassment.

Giving credit where credit's due. We never gave credit. I know so many bar owners who've been caught out big style by the 'tab runners'. These guys can drink. They start going into a bar on a regular basis, usually every night, and will spend a fortune and pay as they go. The bar owner thinks all his birthdays have come at once, as he's never taken so much money. Then, after a few days, once the owner's confidence has built up, they start paying their bill at the end of the night, and then eventually they start a tab, paying every second or third night. The final stage is when the tab has built up to a significant amount and, just like magic, these people disappear, never to be seen again. We knew one lady bar owner who let this get completely out of hand and was taken for tabs to the value of 1,200 euros.

Do not give credit to anyone, ever.

The musicians. Every bar and restaurant, in fact anywhere there are tourists in Spain, gets 'the musicians'. I use the term loosely, as some of them would be better described as comedians. Like the Lookie Lookie men who sell scam trainers, watches, hats and sunglasses (see below), they are a bit like buses: you won't see one for an hour and then ten will turn up within the space of 15 minutes. There's the singer with a guitar, the accordion player, you name it and somebody plays it – usually quite badly.

There was one old guy who used to arrive at the front of the terrace with something resembling a children's Fisher Price battery-operated plastic piano. Just before he started, you'd see him flick a switch at the back and then pretend to press the keys. He'd get quite carried away, exaggerating the key banging when it was obvious he wasn't playing it at all. To make matters worse, the tune was invariably Jingle Bells – just what you want on your annual fortnight's holiday in the middle of August. He couldn't understand why hardly anyone gave him any money, and why nearly everyone would fall about laughing at him.

There was also a guy with a guitar who was a lovely, friendly man but couldn't sing to save his life. He'd sing a song in Spanish – God knows what the words were; I think he made them up – to the tune from the Cornetto advert. But he'd scare the kids so much that people would give him money just to get rid of him.

There's also an Elvis impersonator in Fuengirola who appears only to work evenings. I have to say that he's quite good, but he doesn't take any shit. He'll finish his brief act at the front of a bar terrace and then walk round with a bowl collecting donations, and we've seen him on occasions look into the bowl, pick up the 5 or 10 cents someone's just given him and chuck it back at the donor. Heavy stuff, Elvis. Calm down or you'll be having a heart attack – again.

The Lookie Lookie men. The Lookie Lookie men are as good as gold and really nice, friendly guys. Most of them are from Senegal, and I can say in all honesty that I have never seen any bother whatsoever with these guys. I've had a few watches off them myself, and not had a bad one yet. Oh yes, apart from a Breitling, which I noticed once the Lookie Lookie man had gone was spelt **Brie**tling.

But they haven't quite got the DVDs right yet. The guy will swear blind that the DVD you are purchasing is the one stated on the sleeve, and yes, it is definitely in English. Then you get it home, and it's in Spanish. Some are excellent, but it's not unusual to settle down with a cup of tea or can of beer to enjoy your chosen film, turn it on, the quality's not too bad, it's in English as promised, and then suddenly there's some bloke blocking the picture. It's actually been filmed in the cinema, and some guy's standing up to go to the loo or buy a packet of popcorn.

You have to give the Lookie Lookie men 10 out of 10 for initiative though. They can be there on the seafront one minute, selling watches, sunglasses and CDs, then the heavens open and the rain comes down and, within minutes, the same guys are back on the terrace selling umbrellas. It's fantastic. They must have ammo' dumps hidden around the town for a quick change of merchandise.

Occasionally, the local police will have a clampdown on the Lookie Lookie men and confiscate their merchandise. So from time to time you'd get one of them legging it into the bar, throwing their briefcase full of goods behind the counter, and sauntering out whistling. You knew immediately that the police were around and he'd be back in an hour or so for his case, and off he'd go again.

We went to the Sierra Nevada one day in March to see the ski resort, and there they were, the Lookie Lookie men, selling designer bobble hats and ski gloves. What initiative.

The early-morning drunk. It's a fact of life if you have a café or bar in Spain that occasionally you'll have no sooner put the tables and chairs out in the morning than this character will be sat down, before you even saw him (or her) coming – unshaven, if it's a man, and always grubby and dishevelled looking. Sometimes they'll have come straight from a nightclub, sometimes from the apartment of a girl they met the previous night, and sometimes they won't have a clue where the hell they've been.

'A pint of lager please,' or 'A brandy please.'

We had them all to start with, until I decided to tell anyone who looked the worse for wear first thing in the morning, 'Sorry, but our licence doesn't allow us to sell alcoholic drinks until midday.' Most knew this was rubbish, but what could they do about it? So they'd just get up and stagger further along the promenade and into another place that *would* serve them.

One morning, a young Geordie guy came in first thing and asked how much a coffee would cost – not a good sign if someone doesn't know if they have the price of a coffee. To be fair, he was a nice lad, and it transpired that he didn't know where he was staying. He was over with a friend for just three days, had arrived the previous day, dumped his case in his hotel room and then gone straight to the bar, as he was staying in an 'all-inclusive' hotel. From what he could remember, he'd downed numerous pints of the local rocket fuel and then got a taxi with his friend to Bonanza Square in Benalmadena. They'd then proceeded to drink various loopy cocktails and got split up during the course of the evening. He not only didn't know the name of his hotel, but he didn't even know which resort he was staying in. He had some blood on his shirt and I asked if he'd been fighting. He couldn't remember, but agreed that, by the look of him, if he had, he'd lost.

As it happened, some friends of ours came in shortly afterwards. They'd lived here for quite a few years, so knew a lot more about the geography of the place than we did, and we sat down together and tried to get a few clues.

'If you got a taxi to Bonanza Square in Benalmadena, can you remember how much it cost you? Then we can narrow down the possible position of your hotel.'

'About 10 euros, I think. Although it might have been 20.'

Oh Christ, what a state to get into. Not remembering the name of your hotel is bad enough, but not even knowing which resort you are staying in indicates serious 'power drinking'.

At the time there was only one all-inclusive hotel in Fuengirola, the Gardenia Park, so I'm afraid that was the only help we could offer him. He knew what time he was flying out of Malaga the next day, so I suggested that, as a last resort, he made his way to the airport and waited for his friend to arrive for the flight.

'I can't do that, as I think (hope) that my passport is in the hotel room.'

Off he trots to the Gardenia Park, which is about a two-mile walk, in a brand new pair of rubber flip-flops he'd just bought, as he'd also managed to lose his shoes during the previous night's proceedings.

I would love to know what happened to that guy. If he didn't strike lucky at the Gardenia Park, it would have been a case of hiking to Benalmadena and then on to Torremolinos in flip-flops. 'Power drinking'!

A couple of times, a woman who was probably in her mid-forties came in around 9.30 in the morning, drank a couple of beers and then left. She had a huge nose and a bright red face. Although she wasn't completely scruffy, she certainly wasn't straight out of French Connection's front window. She was usually already half-cut when she came in, and didn't look a full shilling to me, an observation that was soon to be confirmed.

I decided I didn't want her in, and that if she reappeared, I'd refuse to serve her. Sure enough, some time later, she came round the corner first thing in the morning with a 'Kermit the Frog' glove puppet on her right hand. She was talking to this bloody thing as she entered our terrace and sat down. I was that gob-smacked at first that I couldn't react at all; I just froze with my mouth open in complete disbelief.

As I approached her, and before I could say anything, she asked me for a beer.

'Pardon?' I said.

'A beer please.'

Am I imagining this? Is a drunken, middle-aged woman with Kermit stuck on the end of her arm trying to be a ventriloquist and asking for a beer?

'No,' I said. 'I'm not serving you. I'm afraid you'll have to leave.'

'Kermit, this nasty man will not give me a drink. You ask him if you can have a drink then Kermit.'

'Could I have a beer please?' said Kermit.

Like a daft prat, I'm now looking at Kermit instead of her.

'No, I am not serving you,' I said to Kermit.

'Well I want a beer Kermit, you want a beer, and this nasty man will not serve either of us. You've done nothing wrong Kermit. Ask the man again.'

'*Please* can I have a beer?' said Kermit again.

I never intended this to be a negotiation, but I'm sure as hell not going to stand there talking to a f***ing frog.

'Just get out. Go away. Please.'

She then started whispering into Kermit's ear so that I couldn't hear what she was saying. Eventually she got up and wandered off, with Kermit looking over her shoulder telling me what a nasty man I was. All the way across the terrace and for 50 metres down the road I could see Kermit bobbing around over her shoulder and nodding his head, no doubt still bad-mouthing me.

It's funny now, but at the time it ruins your day. You don't need it.

On the odd occasion when someone sat down before we realised they were drunk, I'd have the 'Ken Dodd laugh' with them: 'I bet you can't say this: Ken Dodd's dad's dog's dead. Who killed Ken Dodd's dad's dog?' It's absolutely amazing, but nine times out of ten, someone who's inebriated can say it perfectly. If they're sober, they stammer, stutter and spit all over the place and get nowhere near. Why is that?

There was another guy who came in a few times, and although it would be unfair to say that he was always drunk, he could certainly quaff a fair amount of red wine. Have you ever had the misfortune to know a compulsive liar? Liars tell lies, but compulsive liars tell huge big lies, and this guy took the biscuit. He was a small guy of about 40 years old, with a shaved head and a slight nervous twitch that sometimes made him look as if he was rapidly winking at everyone. After a couple of visits, he told us he'd been a paratrooper in the British Army and had served in just about every country you care to name.

The next time he came in, he'd obviously been on the wine, and had apparently forgotten about this conversation, as this time he told us he was ex-SAS. He prattled on about the army and then suddenly turned to me and said, 'Have you ever killed anybody?' Funnily enough, it wasn't a question that required a great deal of thought, so I just said 'No.'

'Oh, I've killed lots of people in my time; both service kills and private.'

'Oh, really? That's nice.'

'Yeah, but the worst one was when I had to kill my best mate.'

'Oh, that must have been terrible,' I said.

'Yeah, he was badly injured and in a lot of pain, so he asked me to finish him off. I shot him through the head and carried on advancing. But it affected me badly'.

Well it would do wouldn't it – if it was true.

I'd more or less forgotten about this guy when up he popped again a few days later. We weren't very busy at the time, and he sat at one of the front tables. I knew I was in for some more elaborate tales, but it was even worse this time.

'You know the other day when I told you I had to kill my best mate?'

Yawn, 'Yes I do.'

'Well, that was bad enough, but it wasn't really the worst kill I've had to make.' 'Oh really?' I said cautiously.

'No. I once had to kill my dog, and he was a better mate to me than my best mate was.'

I knew I was going to have to listen to this, come what may, so I just asked him how that came about.

'Well,' he said, 'it was a German Shepherd dog and he got run over but not killed. He dragged his way back to my flat and I couldn't see him suffer. (*Pity he didn't feel the same sympathy for me.*) So I just kissed him, put my hands around his neck and strangled him right there and then on the floor. I cried afterwards, but I'm sure the dog would have thanked me for what I did.'

Have you ever tried to strangle a German Shepherd dog? No, I guess not. But come on. I had to disappear into the kitchen as I was cracking up with laughter, and I didn't dare let him see me in case I was the next one to feel his hands around my throat.

Once I'd recovered and went back out onto the terrace, he told me that he was now a mercenary in Africa. The number of African countries he'd apparently saved from revolutionaries was unbelievable, and I didn't even recognise the names of some of them – largely because they don't exist. In fairness, he was a bit more hammered than usual, and that was probably why he got even more carried away than on previous occasions. But the interesting thing is that I honestly believe he thought it was all true.

So, as you can see, there's rarely a dull moment in this game. Every day is different, not least because of the eccentricities of the people you meet.

Do you still fancy having a bar in Spain? Read on.

Chapter 6

Buying a bar: the options

It's easy isn't it? If I buy a bar, I can sit in the sun all day and everyone will want to come into it, won't they' *No.*

There are so many horror stories about Brits who come over here, jump straight in, don't understand how it all works, have no business sense whatsoever, and go home skint after six months.

If you're considering buying a bar, café or restaurant in Spain, the first thing is to be aware of the three main options available to you.

1. Buying an existing freehold

It depends how deep your pockets are, but if money isn't an issue, buying the freehold on an already successful bar is obviously the best investment. However, these are difficult to find, and very expensive if they're any good, as the freehold owners don't generally want to sell them.

2. Buying the freehold on an empty unit

The second option is to buy an empty unit underneath a brand new apartment complex. These are also expensive and fairly difficult to find, as the Spanish tend to purchase them 'off plan' before building has even commenced. By doing this, they buy at a much cheaper price than would be the case for a finished building. They then sell the lease, usually to a Brit.

However, the downside of purchasing or leasing a brand new unit is the fact that it's completely and utterly empty, a shell. You then have to install all the electrics, tables, chairs, chillers, cookers… You're into serious money here, which is why most people go for the third option.

3. Leasing

It's no exaggeration to say that there are very few bars in Spain that are not for sale at the right price (for the lease, that is). However, if you walk around any of the main tourist resorts, you'll hardly ever see a 'For sale' sign outside a bar or restaurant. That is not the way it's usually done.

Whichever route you decide to take, if you buy or lease a business, make sure you use an ***independent*** *gestoria* and/or solicitor. (A *gestoria* is a cross between an accountant and a solicitor and will sort out all the bureaucracy for you.) Agents and owners will tell you that in order to make things easier, you should use their *gestoria*/solicitor, but my advice would be to find your own to avoid any conflict of interests. If you have an independent *gestoria*/solicitor who has no attachment to the agent or owner, he'll be able to give you unbiased advice. The contract will be in Spanish, so it's important to have someone you can rely on to tell you about anything in it that might have a negative impact on you. Ask around, look in the local newspapers; there are hundreds of perfectly good ones. So that's the first step.

Under no circumstances sign *anything* unless you are absolutely 100% certain that your *gestoria*/solicitor has seen and understood the content of the contract or agreement. The 'Go on, trust me' factor *must* be dismissed, no matter what. This may sound a bit cynical, but just assume that everyone is out to rob you, and you can then be pleasantly surprised if you find they're not. You'll be told that a bar has a music licence when it doesn't, that it has a lifetime lease when in fact it has a five-year lease – the list is endless. Get it confirmed; be sure.

Bars are usually sold through agents. Unfortunately, most potential bar purchasers arrive in Spain having left their brains on the plane. They haven't a clue what they're looking for, and if they've not already contacted one or more bar agents through the Internet prior to coming over, they read the local English newspapers and contact them once they're here. As in any walk of life, there is good and bad, and in the case of the bar agents over here, there are some really bad ones. Some of them are unqualified, unimpressive and, in certain cases, completely incompetent, and they simply ooze insincerity. Some are failed ex-bar owners themselves who have been previously striped by an agent, learnt the hard way, and probably thought, 'What the hell. I've been done and I now know how I've been done, so I'll just go and do a few Brits myself.' At the end of the day, most of them are only interested in their commission, and will quite happily sell you a complete and utter dog. Obviously not all are out of this mould, and there are some very good agents (I think). But how can you tell the good from the bad?

There's no easy answer to this question. It's really no different from in the UK, in that you have to rely on your own instincts and common sense, and perhaps on any recommendations or warnings you're able to pick up locally. For example, there's one bar agent in Fuengirola who's referred to by just about everyone in the bar/café trade as 'Dodgy Bob', which is the type of information it might be useful for a newcomer to the area to have!

But, as much as people hate the agents, there are often good reasons why sellers use them. When a lease owner sells a lease, he has to pay the freehold owner between 10% and 30% of the selling price, depending on the agreement – 20% of the selling price is the norm on transfer to the new lease owner. As often as not, what happens is that the existing lease owner will tell the freehold owner that he's selling the bar for considerably less than the actual price agreed, thus only having to pay out 20% of a lower figure. If the existing leaseholder sticks a 'For sale' sign outside the bar, the freehold owner will probably send a friend round pretending to be interested in buying the lease. The friend will enquire about the price, and bingo, scam revealed. Once the freehold owner knows what the actual selling price is, he wants his full 20%. If, on the other hand, the leaseholder sells through an agent, the freehold owner doesn't even know the bar is for sale (no sign).

The costs of leases vary dramatically, but say, for example, that the actual sale price is 72,000 euros; the leaseholder will declare he is selling the business for, say, 43,000 euros. He has immediately saved 20% of the 29,000 euros difference – nearly six grand, thank you very much. Then, when the transaction is made, the 29,000 euros difference will be paid direct to the seller by the purchaser in the form of a briefcase full of cash. But there's a trap that people fall into here. The freehold owner has first option on buying back the lease. So when a lease owner informs the freehold owner that he's selling the bar, the freehold owner has the right to say, 'Well that's quite cheap. I'm prepared to pay that and buy it back from you myself.' So if you tell him a price that's obviously too cheap, he may call your bluff and buy it back at your deflated 'blag' price, and you have lost out.

It works like this. You buy the lease and then pay a monthly rent for the life of your lease, which is usually five years. At the time of writing, based on a standard bar or restaurant unit, the lease will cost you between about 30,000 and 115,000 euros. This cost can be looked upon as an investment, as you hope that if you've paid that much for it, someone else will pay the same or more in the future when you sell.

Five-year and ten-year leases are often (not always) guaranteed as renewable to you if you want to stay, a fact that will/should be written into the contract together with the maximum percentage by which the rent can be increased for the second five or ten years.

Buying a bar or restaurant in Spain is no different from buying a house or business in the UK in the respect of location, location, location. But even more important is the rent. Believe me, if the rent's not right, you're dead, moribund, out for the count, skint, on a plane home, before you even open the door of your bar on the first day.

If you buy the lease for a bar in a back street for the lower 30,000 euros, you'll probably live to wish you hadn't. As much as you might think that people will come into your place, the chances are they won't. If you go for a front-line promenade location, you'll pay considerably more for the lease; it will be the top end of the price bracket plus some, depending on size and location. But although the lease will cost you more, you are going to get more passing trade: holidaymakers will always walk along the seafront.

However, even a prime location on the seafront doesn't guarantee success. It certainly helps, but look at how many other units there are in the immediate vicinity. Are they British? Dutch? Spanish? What are they doing and how busy are they? If there are a few units doing what you intend to do, then remember that you'll only be diluting the business that's already there. Also, if there *are* other similar businesses, the chances are that there will already be a price war going on. So, to stand any chance whatsoever, you'll have to be cleaner, better and have more personality than the existing businesses.

Decide what you want to do before you start looking. Is it a bar you want? A café? A restaurant? Do you prefer to work evenings or days? Too many Brits don't really know what they want to do. They look around and find a business they think they like and then carry on exactly as the previous owners did. In all likelihood, these people were not making enough money to make it pay – hence the sale to you.

There's a list of questions you need to ask the agent with regard to the life of the lease on the property you're interested in, including the following.

- Is it guaranteed renewable to you after the stated period?
- Are all licences in place?
- Is the rent inclusive of IVA (VAT)?
- Are community charges etc. included in the rent?

Again, don't just rely on the verbal answers you're given to these questions; you must have them confirmed in writing before signing the contract, which is another reason for having an independent *gestoria*/solicitor.

When you purchase a business, you won't be looking at audited books; it doesn't work like that here. All you'll have is 'the word' of the owner and/or agent. Assume this to be a complete lie, because it probably is. Owners declare as little as possible about their turnover, and therefore any figures you look at will be made up. In any case, they aren't really all that important. Even if you're lucky enough to take over a business that did have accurate books (which is very unlikely), it isn't what the existing owner takes that matters: it's what you do with the business.

Remember, there's very little 'goodwill' here. If you bought a café or bar in the UK, you'd probably inherit regular customers who'd continue to come if you maintained or exceeded the standards of the previous owners. In a Spanish holiday resort, you have very few regular all-year-round customers. By definition, you are catering for holidaymakers, who'll visit you a few times during their one or two weeks of holiday and then disappear, probably never to be seen again. If you're really lucky, you'll catch a couple or a family on their first or second day, they'll like your products and service, and hopefully come in every day for the rest of their holiday. But even then, you'll only get a week or two out of them, at best.

In order to illustrate to you just how lacking in common sense some people can be, read on.

We came into contact with a couple from London who'd come over to Spain and wanted to buy a tourist bar. They were adamant that they wouldn't use an agent, as they'd heard from someone in the UK that agents slam a large commission fee on top of the owner's asking price (usually about 10%, but it can be more). So, knowing that everyone has their price, they decided they'd do the deal themselves.

This couple spent quite a few weeks doing what was in essence a pub-crawl around Benalmadena, Fuengirola, Nirja, La Cala, Calahonda… They were looking, listening and generally doing all the right things, as well as presumably getting off their heads most days in the name of research. They narrowed things down until finally deciding they wanted to buy a particular bar in Fuengirola. I will never know why they chose this specific bar, as, although it's very nice, it's not in a particularly good place for volume business.

They began to frequent this bar regularly and became quite friendly with the lease owner. After a while the guy struck.

'I would like to buy your bar. How much would you sell it for?'

'Make me an offer,' the owner replied.

'£75,000,' the guy said.

Now, I happen to know that the bar owner paid £35,000 for the lease from someone who couldn't get out quick enough. So obviously he snapped this guy's hand off: done, sold, thank you very much.

The rent on this place was 1,200 euros per month, and nobody was going to make a good living out of it. Needless to say, the couple are now struggling like hell and wanting to sell, as they are haemorrhaging money every week. The guy wanted this particular bar for whatever reason, and was obviously determined to get it. But the moral of the story is: don't go straight in with a big offer. If he does manage to sell it now, he'll probably have to take an amount close to the original £35,000. So he'll have lost 40 grand Sterling, plus all the money he's spent running the place during his time of occupation.

Some people do well out of running bars, restaurants and cafés in Spain, but many more lose thousands of pounds. So don't get carried away. Take your time to look around, at different times of the day; do your research thoroughly and, however tempting, don't allow yourself to be guided by misplaced optimism.

Chapter 7

Doing the sums

Businesses sell for widely different amounts of money, and rents vary dramatically, but in order to illustrate a typical scenario, I've created a hypothetical situation.

Let's take 'Dave and Sue Average'. They sell their semi-detached house in the UK, pay off their mortgage, settle up with everyone else (or not!), and have, say, £50,000 in their pocket – a lot of money to most people.

Their flight lands in Spain, and they leave their brains on the plane.

Dave and Sue rent an apartment, room or whatever, and are being shown numerous bars by the agents. With 50 grand, you might think you're loaded, but it soon goes if you're not earning. To the agents, Dave and Sue represent a dream come true: they don't know the form, they don't know the geography, and they have little or no business sense. Have we got the ideal property for them!

If Dave and Sue arrive with £50,000, they'll struggle badly to buy the lease on a decent bar and still have money to live on. So they'll inevitably finish up with a bar that is a complete no-hoper, for reasons no one who'd just got off a plane from the UK would ever even consider. They'll be shown what are called 'starter bars'. That's a laugh! They should call them 'suicide bars', because whoever buys them usually finishes up either completely skint and suicidal or, at the very least, a divorced alcoholic.

But let's try to be positive to start with. Dave and Sue are horrified by the price of bars on the seafront. They can't afford this location, so they buy the lease on a starter bar for, say, 45,000 euros. That's a big chunk of their well-earned money gone straightaway. Once they get the keys, they find the electrics are shot, the chill cabinet doesn't work, the chairs are held together with string, and there's a full housing estate of cockroaches in residence. It's not what it appeared to be is it? 'But here we are. We'll have to make the best of it and get these things fixed.' That means another two grand at least – that's 47,000 euros out of their original £50,000 already gone.

The rub is the rent. Strangely enough, the rent on a rubbish starter bar is often the same as, and in some cases more than, the rent for a good bar. *This is engineered; it's done on purpose.*

Let's think this through. If you own the freehold on a bar or restaurant and it's in a position where you know it has not been, is not, and will not ever be a good business, you can sell the lease quite cheaply. There's always someone who can't afford the going rate for a good one. Once you've sold your relatively cheap lease, you then charge a high rent. It's unbelievable that many people think it's great to get a bar for a cheap price (for the lease, that is), but they don't think about the rent. If you're paying a high rent for a business in a bad location, you're chasing stars, big numbers, all day, all week, all month.

But having left their brains and common sense on the plane, many people don't even consider this aspect. You can easily generate a rough business plan for a bar or restaurant on the back of a cigarette packet or beer mat – does it stack up financially?

The following would be typical costs for an average starter bar with a cheap lease.

Cost of lease: say 45,000 Euros cash outlay.

The following figures are overheads **per week** (in Euros), based on 28 working days per month.

The bar	
Rent	250
Electricity/gas	60
Gestoria (accountant)	31
Terrace Tax	32*
Bar insurance	14
National Insurance (2 people)	110
IVA on rent (VAT to us)	35**
Company/Personal Tax	30
Repairs and renewals	20***
Refuse/bins	2

Pest control	6
Total	**590**

*You must accrue for your Terrace Tax. If you have an outside terrace, you'll be hit with a significant bill once a year. In Fuengirola, this is presently payable in May, so if you buy a business early in the year, the bill will hit you soon. Terrace Tax varies depending on the square metres (area of your terrace) and, as an example, ours was 1,800 euros per annum. A big hit if you're not expecting it!

I can't comment about other Spanish towns, but in Fuengirola, if you can prove that you live in the town itself, you get a 30% reduction on Terrace Tax, which is well worth having.

You should also accrue for IVA (VAT). The freehold owner has to pay IVA on the rent he/she collects, which at present is at a rate of 20%. In reality, this is collected from **you, and you need to be aware of it, as it is yet another cost to your business.

***Allow for repairs and renewals, as you will always have a chill cabinet requiring a new motor or thermostat or a microwave packing in – something will happen. We had to get new scissor gates on the front of our unit, which cost 1,000 euros. If you're not accruing for repairs and renewals, this is a big whack to anyone.

You also have to live of course!

Home	
Apartment rent	200*
Apartment electricity and water	15
Petrol	20
Car insurance	12
Mobile phone	30
Shopping	120
Total	**397**

*800 euros per month gets you a decent, furnished, two-bed apartment on an 11-month contract.

Grand total (bar + home)	**987**

That's near enough 1,000 euros per week that you'll need to take just in order to stand still – but don't forget about your stock. You have to buy stock in order to sell it. Work on around 30% of your turnover going to pay for the stock, although this will depend on what you sell, i.e. drinks only, drinks and snacks etc.

So, including stock, that takes it, in round figures, to **1,300 euros per week** you require just to stand still. No going out for a drink, the odd meal, buying clothes, shoes, holidays. You need to add on some more for all of that. So add it on – you're only fooling yourself if you don't!

Don't forget also that if you do take a holiday, it's a 'double whammy'. Not only do you have to accrue for the cost of the holiday, you also lose the takings for its duration. You are not working for someone else now you know.

The costs above also assume that a couple are going to run the business on their own, with no paid help or staff. Can you manage that?

One last point: your opening licence will cost you, in round figures, 1,000 euros, so don't forget to allow for that too.

Okay, let's now see how many punters we need to generate the necessary revenue.

You can pitch the average spend where you like, but do not underestimate the number of people you'll get in who will only buy one drink – a beer, a coffee, a soft drink. When you come to do your calculations, you can increase the 3 euros per person average spend I've used below if you want to, but don't kid yourself.

Turnover

(A)   Assume 50 customers per day, each spending an average of 3 euros =150 euros per day. That gives you 900 euros per week based on working six days.

(B)   Assume 100 customers per day, each spending an average of 3 euros = 300 euros per day. That gives you 1,800 euros per week based on working six days.

Obviously, turnover (A) is nowhere near enough. Turnover (B) is not a bad little business – not great, but not bad.

The fact is that if you're behind the front line on a back street where there are inevitably other competing bars, you haven't got a cat in hell's chance of getting 100 customers in per day. Don't kid yourself. Forget it. You're bust.

What about the winter months? We know of so-called starter bars in Fuengirola and Benalmadena that are lucky to get eight or ten people in a day – and in the winter they may not get any. It's amazing how many people buy bars without doing simple sums and then can't understand why they're losing money hand over fist. Many do not have deep pockets, and when they fall behind with the rent, they try to sell on the lease. If they can't sell quickly, they have no option but to put the keys back through the letterbox – and the 45,000 euros or whatever they paid for the lease is gone. In the case of 'Dave and Sue Average', their living expenses have also come out of their original £50,000 and they're on a plane back to the UK, completely broke.

Freehold owner: 'Thank you very much. Next please!'

I knew a guy who only recently sold his lease on a good bar and secured a very good price for it. With the money, he bought the freehold on a completely empty unit under an apartment block down a back street. The unit had been bricked up for years and the existing owner just wanted rid of it, so he was able to purchase the freehold for a song. This guy then proceeded to turn the unit into an extremely nice little bar. He knew where to go for fairly cheap furniture and also who to use for building the bar area, toilets etc. It looks nice, very nice, and he's now (during the winter) trying to sell the lease for a very reasonable price, but has deliberately fixed the rent at a high level. To some innocent coming over here with a limited budget, it would appear to be a cheap lease price for a very nice, brand new bar. They will be told that 'during the summer months these streets are heaving with tourists' and that it's an excellent starter bar. In reality, there is no way the bar will take enough money to cover the high rent, running costs and living costs – not a hope in hell.

Six months, nine months, it won't take long. The innocent new lease owner will run out of money and give the keys back to the freehold owner because he won't be able to afford the rent any more. Thank you very much – re-sell the lease in winter and away we go again. The bar's a cash cow, and there's a hell of a good living to be made out of this type of deal if you don't have any problems sleeping at night.

So, if you are thinking of buying a bar or restaurant in Spain, do the sums. Sit across the road for a couple of hours at different times every day. Watch not only the business in question, but also the street. How many people are passing? Are they predominantly tourists? Are there any busy bars in that street? If so, what's so special about what they do? It's not unknown for sellers to rent a crowd for the visit of a potential buyer. If you look at a bar and it's full of customers, go back a few times. Don't fall for the oldest trick in the book.

Keep a reserve. Whatever happens, make sure you have a slush fund stashed away somewhere for a rainy day (or ten). It will come, believe me. There are always things cropping up that you hadn't allowed for, as well as the bad weeks when you don't cover your costs. And don't think in hundreds of pounds: you'll need at least a few thousand as a backup, and if you don't have it, you're bust.

There are more failures than successes, and very few bars, cafés or restaurants see out the standard five-year lease: they either sell the lease on or go bust and hand back the keys.

Do the sums.
Don't get carried away with your fag-packet business plan, however good it might seem after a few beers!

Of course, not everyone plays by the rules. There are numerous bars and restaurants in Spain that are illegal: no opening licence, no music licence, owners and staff not paying National Insurance etc. These are risks people sometimes take because they have no choice, i.e. they're not taking enough money through the front door to pay for legalities and simply can't afford them.

So, having dealt with all the problems mentioned so far and avoided all the pitfalls of getting your bar, café or restaurant, let's assume you buy a good little business. One thing I would not recommend is cutting down your potential audience. Many people do this without realising it. Take a Yorkshire couple who want to call their bar 'The Yorkshire Boy' – 'That'll attract Yorkshire people like us, won't it?' Well, yes, possibly. But it may also put off any Lancastrian, Londoner, Scot or anyone from any of the other non-Yorkshire regions of the UK. Then there's the Scottish couple who decide to call their bar 'The Scotsman'. The same applies. The name is extremely important, and narrowing your clientele is not a good idea.

The last thing I want to do is put people off from coming over to Spain and buying a business. However, it is important to have an insight into some of the traps you can fall into. I wish I'd been able to learn something about how it really is before we moved to Spain. We've met numerous people who've bought businesses over here and succeeded, but, to repeat myself – there are far more failures than successes.

Chapter 8

Just some of the things that can go wrong

One day we were working in our teashop when a young couple came in. We were fairly quiet at the time, so we got talking. They were asking various questions about our business and then said they'd just bought a bar. They were very excited about it, and I asked them where it was. As soon as they told me, I knew the place, and my heart sank for them. It's a long row of bars that people refer to as 'the garages' and 'suicide row', and in fact they do resemble a long row of garages. I've never counted them, but I'd say there are probably 18 or maybe 20 bars doing more or less the same thing.

The units change hands at a frightening rate. They face a car park, apart from the five or six units in the centre of the row, which look out over rather untidy spare land. The wire fence surrounding the spare land is about four metres from the front entrance of these bars, so the view is, to say the least, not good. Also, in order to get to one of these middle bars, you have to walk through the neighbouring bars. Forget it; you're dead before you open. Who the hell is going to walk through other bars just to get to you, unless it's your best mate?

This couple went on to tell me that they'd bought this ´starter bar´ through an agent – and that it was in the centre of the row. Oh hell! Both the seller and the agent had told them that the spare land was to be landscaped by the council – honest. They also told them that once the landscaping was complete, the council would give these bars a few metres of the new gardens to put tables on. 'That will make all the difference in the world, won't it?'

They were so excited, and I didn't know whether to laugh or cry. These poor people had fallen for the lot, and had just thrown their money down the drain. On the odd occasion I went past the garages after that, I'd look over and see them sitting on their own, waiting for customers who didn't arrive. A few months later the bar was locked up – and they were gone.

A similar thing happened a while later when another couple started to come in to the teashop on a regular basis. After a few conversations, it came out that they'd bought a starter bar and would be getting the keys in a week or so. When they told me which street it was on, I thought, 'Oh Christ no; you're dead.' We actually got to know these people quite well and, once they opened, Chris and I went round a couple of times for a drink to support them, and there was never anyone in. They'd sit there from 10.00 a.m. until midnight, every day. One week they took 10 euros – in the whole week – and the writing was on the wall.

It was actually quite a nice little bar, but in completely the wrong place. Hardly anyone went down that street, and if they did, they were invariably local Spanish people – and the last thing *they* would do is go into a British bar, where the prices are generally higher because the customers are tourists. Three months, at most, and they were shafted. Unfortunately, the situation actually split them up and he went back to the UK. The lady stayed for a while and tried to get a job, but things didn't work out, and she also had to go back to the UK in the end. It's a very sad story, because she's a lovely lady who just bought the wrong business.

Chris and I went to a bar for a drink early one evening and got talking to a father and son. They told us they'd bought a bar on the seafront in Torreblanca, which is at the far eastern end of Fuengirola. They'd only been in this bar for three weeks and were extremely disappointed at the number of people they were getting in. But they were sure things would pick up shortly, as there appeared to be a lot of people walking past, going to and from the large hotel nearby. Oh dear! They obviously hadn't done their homework, and I didn't have the heart to tell them that that particular hotel is *all inclusive*. If they'd looked at the passing people more closely, they'd have seen that most of them were wearing little plastic wristbands. Why would they go into this bar when they could stay in their hotel and get completely legless for free?

Another example – there are lots of them – is of a guy who actually escaped disaster. He was a cockney who started coming into our place asking all kinds of questions about running a bar/café, and was anxious to buy one as soon as possible. Sure enough, a couple of days later, he came in all excited and told me he'd seen the perfect place, 'right on the seafront, with lots of tables. Yes, this is the one.'

He explained which bar it was, and as he had not yet paid a deposit, I said to him, 'Look, I won't advise you, but if you don't mind I will point something out to you.'

'Sure,' he said, 'please do.'

'I know this bar you're so excited about. It's not the normal seafront-type bar with a terrace directly outside the front door. It doesn't have a canopy over it with canvas sides, which you can drop down in the rain or wind. All its tables are out on the actual pavement, and there is no way you can put up a canopy. All you have are sun umbrellas over each individual table.'

'Yes,' he said, 'that's the one.'

'Well, that's fine on hot summer days. But what do you do when it rains or if it's a windy day? You know – winter.'

'I don't know. I hadn't thought about that.'

'I'll tell you what you do – you shut. You have no option. Who in their right mind is going to sit under a sun umbrella in the rain or when it's windy? There will be lots of days like that in the winter and you will have no income whatsoever.'

'Oh, thanks for that,' he said – and he didn't buy that bar.

Think it through!

Of course, some failures occur due to pure bad luck. Two gay guys took over a bar where Chris and I sometimes went for a drink after work. They wanted it to be a family bar, and they cleaned, painted and generally did it up so that it was immaculate. All was going well and they built up a good little business. But unfortunately, shortly after they'd taken over, the council turned up one day and dug up the whole road outside, pavements and all. No warning, no compensation, nothing. Overnight, the nice tree-lined avenue at the front of their sun terrace became a holding area for huge concrete pipes and JCBs. It absolutely decimated their turnover for months, and it's something you'd never consider looking into prior to signing the lease – are there any serious road works about to begin? Fortunately, they also had an entrance at the rear (so to speak), so they managed to ride it out, but they struggled badly.

Along the same road as our friends' bar, there are two other British-owned bars, but these have only one entrance, at the front. So when the roads and pavements were ripped up, it was an obstacle course just trying to enter these bars. Their turnover ground to a halt immediately, and when they enquired about how long the work would take, they were told that storm drains were being installed and that it would take six months – ish.

Now, if you are chasing 1,100 euros per month rent, National Insurance, all your other fixed costs, plus your own living expenses, you need very deep pockets to see yourself through six months with virtually no turnover. What can you do about it? Nothing. You either have the money in the bank to be able to subsidise yourself for six months – ish – or you do not. If you don't, you're bust, and the money you invested in the lease (say £60,000) is lost forever. If you were unfortunate enough to have bought a bar just prior to the road works, your chances of selling it when outside looks like a scene from a Dresden street circa 1945 are nil.

We knew another couple who bought a bar in a back street. They were convinced they would attract customers, as the husband was a singer and entertainer, but they opened up without looking into the legalities of having live music on the premises. Away they go, blaring live music out every night until daft o'clock and, surprise, surprise, the neighbours were not happy at all. The police turned up one night, closed them down immediately, and padlocked their door: 'You need a music licence for that you know.' They lost the lot.

Of course, added to all the things that can go wrong, there are a lot of things you can do to make them worse.

One common mistake made by bar and café owners when they realise it's not quite as easy as they first thought and are wondering what they can do in order to improve things and get people to come in, is to decide, 'I know, I'll be cheaper than all the other places around me.' Unless you can purchase stock a lot cheaper than anyone else, which you can't, the only way to make a half-decent profit out of selling cheap is to sell in *volume*.

The average bar or café in Spain is relatively small: if you have 20 people in, you're quite busy. On that basis, volume isn't an option. If you reduce your prices by, say, 20%, you require a considerable number of extra customers just to make the same money. Then there's the extra legwork on the terrace, washing up, cooking etc. The chances are that if you did reduce your prices by 20%, you wouldn't generate enough extra customers to justify the price reduction. In other words, you'd be working harder for less money.

Then there's *the loss leader* – what's that all about? A café bar just along the promenade from us started selling a pint of lager for 1 euro when the going rate was around 2 euros 50 cents. I was talking to the owner one day and asked him his train of thought on this 1 euro pint. 'Oh that's a loss leader,' he told me. 'The 1 euro pint will pull them in and then they'll order a meal or a sandwich.' Every time I walked past this place it was packed, but when I looked closely I could see that everyone in there was just drinking – who wouldn't be, at a pint of lager for 1 euro a chuck? Two weeks later, the price was back up to the normal level.

Certain beer suppliers will give you a free barrel every fifth or sixth barrel purchased, and, every now and again, you'll see a large sign outside a bar: 'Buy a pint and get the second pint free.' How stupid can you get? You get a free barrel from the brewery and then you give it away to holidaymakers who you're never likely to see again. It's not as though there's goodwill and close customer relationships to consider here, as would be the case with locals at a UK pub. That's just not good business sense.

Actually, if you are quiet, there's a good argument for putting your prices UP! Take a look at your prices every now and again: an extra 10 cents here and 20 cents there on tea, coffee, a sandwich can make quite a difference over a week, and the chances are that you won't lose any customers because of it.

As with any business, people will pay for quality and cleanliness. So, rather than serving tea in a grubby mug with a teabag floating on top, use individual pots. Serve a sandwich with a small salad garnish. Make sure your toilets are always clean. People will gladly pay that little bit extra, and the chances are that they'll come back the following day.

If you have a bar or café, you'll receive some kind or delivery or other during the course of most days. It's sod's law that the delivery will arrive when you're busy and you'll just point to where you want them to leave it, look at the price on the invoice, pay the guy as quickly as possible, and then get on with what you were doing. Very often, a little later, when things have slowed down, you'll check the invoice against the delivery and bang – a case of drinks short, a pack of cheese short, something. Watch these people; they try it on.

And talking of trust… It isn't only buying the lease on a bar in Spain that can land you in trouble. We knew a guy – I'll call him John to save his blushes – who was a cook and who had been considering buying a bar or café but just couldn't find the right place. He started frequenting an evening bar that didn't offer food, and got chatting to the owner. After a while, this guy asked John what he thought about the idea of kitting out the existing storeroom as a kitchen and running the place as a café during the day, leaving the owner to carry on running the bar in the evenings. The plan was to split the daytime food takings three ways: a third for the owner as rent, a third for John, and the remaining third for food stock. The proceeds of any drink sales during the day would go to the owner too – so not a bad proposition for him then.

John thought it was worth a try, as it would give him a feel for running a café in Spain and would also save him the cost of buying a lease.

Then came the rub. The bar owner told John that he didn't mind paying for fitting out the kitchen, as it would enhance his property, but he didn't have the cash at the present time. ('No, John, walk away,' I hear you cry.) But John dipped into his savings and offered to lend the owner the money. I didn't ever ask him how much, but we have to be talking 10,000 to 15,000 euros.

After only a few weeks, the bar owner began to come in every day for his (free) lunch, usually choosing the most expensive meal on the menu – sirloin steak, gammon, prawn salad. Thanks very much. But what was more worrying for John was that he started to notice a change in the owner's attitude towards him. The guy was often quite rude and aggressive, and when John began asking him when he was going to start paying back the money for the kitchen, their relationship deteriorated even further until the situation became intolerable and John and the bar parted company. Needless to say, John never got his money back – 'And he seemed such a nice man.'

Trust no one.

Chapter 9

Your accountant – your new best friend

In the UK, people generally play by the rules. Okay, some people may bend them a bit, but there's not a lot you can get away with if you work for a living.

The best advice I can give you if you have any sort of business in Spain, is that you have to have a *gestoria*. He can fast track documents that it would take you as an individual forever to sort out, particularly if you don't speak Spanish. *Gestorias* do very well out of us Brits. Many speak perfect English, as it's obviously in their interests to do so – the Brits are good customers.

You have to live in Spain for quite a while before you realise fully just how much bureaucracy there is here. You go to one place to sort something out and are then sent somewhere else, where you're directed to another office. At each stage you'll queue for eternity, and the chances are that when you finally get near the front of the queue for the correct desk, at the correct office, it will just be closing for *siesta*.

There are bureaucracy, red tape and queues for almost everything.

Life is so different here, and the rules are completely different. In fact, sometimes there are no rules, and if they do exist, nobody quite knows what they are.

A guy we knew who had a bar long before we bought our teashop was doing okay, and one day he said to his *gestoria*, 'I have this friend (honest) who also has a bar and he was wondering whether he should give his *gestoria* **all** his receipts at the end of each month, or if he should sort them out and throw a few in the bin?'

The *gestoria* smiled knowingly and replied, 'No, you should give me all the receipts and I will decide which ones to throw in the bin.'

The same guy wanted a mortgage for an apartment he'd decided to buy, and he and his *gestoria* sat down and discussed how much the property was, how much deposit he could pay, and how much he needed to borrow, and, based on these figures, the *gestoria* said that there'd be no problem.

The guy then said, 'But my business doesn't make a profit on paper. How can you get me a mortgage based on the earnings from a bad business?'

'Oh don't worry about that,' the *gestoria* said. 'I'll pump your profit up for a couple of months and, once the mortgage is issued, I'll take the profit back down again.'

Eh? Can you see an accountant in the UK doing that?

It is not that any particular *gestoria* or solicitor is bent; that's just the way it is. Any dodge is fair game, and that's why there is so much so-called 'black money' in Spain – cash, euro notes, and lots of them. People are walking out of banks all the time with piles of cash to pay the 'black' proportion of a purchase.

Another bar owner we knew, who had a completely different *gestoria*, had a dilemma, as his wife was going back to the UK for two weeks to visit the family. As they ran the bar together, this meant that they either had to close or bring someone in just for the two-week period. So, rather than losing two weeks' turnover, he chose the latter option. Now, this guy was quite unusual for down here, as he played everything straight down the line, by the book. He wouldn't take any chances, and absolutely everything was completely above board and legal.

He spoke to his *gestoria* and told him that he was bringing in a lady to help just for two weeks, but how could he do this, as he didn't want someone from the Town Hall walking in and asking to see her employment contract? His *gestoria* just shrugged and said, 'Give me the name and NIE number (National Insurance) of this person. What I will do is draw up a temporary employment contract and keep it on my desk for the two weeks. Then, if someone walks in, her employment is perfectly legal. However, if nobody walks in, give me a call after the two-week period and I will just rip up the contract and it didn't exist.' 'Err, okay. That's sorted then.'

Whatever you do in Spain, get a good *gestoria* – it's vital.

(This must be the shortest chapter in the book. I wonder why it's so difficult to find much of interest to say about accountants, even when what you *are* saying is all good?)

Chapter 10
Apartments and houses: buying and renting

As I mentioned near the beginning of this book, when people move to Spain, they need to be aware of the things to look and listen for when renting or buying property. You probably won't know the areas, just as you probably wouldn't know the areas if you moved to a different town or city in the UK, but it's astonishing how many people come over to Spain for just a week or two in order to buy property. It's likely to be the second biggest investment you ever make, or, if you're moving to Spain permanently, possibly *the* biggest investment. Obviously, some of the things you need to look out for are the same as in the UK, but others are different.

Mortgages
As mentioned again later in the book, the concept of customer service hasn't yet been widely accepted in Spain, particularly in relation to Spanish banks. It'll all be very friendly when you first approach them, and you'll probably be seen by an English-speaking member of staff, but, further down the line, if and when you have a problem or query, it'll be a case of taking your place in the long queue with everyone else. If you can't speak Spanish, you're likely just to be wafted away, depending on the mood of the cashier. (I use 'cashier' in the singular advisedly here, because, however long the queues, there's likely to be just the one.) So, if you're prepared to take sandwiches and a thermos flask to sustain you while you sort out any problems at the bank, then fine, by all means use one. But I wouldn't recommend it at the moment. If your real-estate agent or *gestoria*/solicitor points you in the direction of a Spanish bank, just keep these comments in mind.

There are some banks, such as Sol Bank, that cater for ex-pats and many of whose staff are fluent English speakers. They make a genuine effort to bring Brits on board, having realised they have an awful lot of money to spend. But there are also some really bad ones (I probably shouldn't name any names here), including one that doesn't (and won't) send out statements, and another that obviously incorporates 'obnoxious attitude' lessons into its staff training sessions.

So, if you do need a mortgage to buy your property, it's probably a good idea to look around and ask some questions before deciding on which bank to approach.

Agents

It's not uncommon for real-estate agents to charge 10% commission, or sometimes more, for a sale. As with anywhere else, there are some perfectly good real-estate agents, and some fairly unscrupulous ones. But, as with the bar agents, how the hell do you know the difference? Probably a good rule of thumb is to be sceptical about everything an agent tells you, unless and until you're able to check it out yourself.

The first thing you need to do is to ask the agent or seller the right questions (with the help of this book). Of course, they may not know the answers, in which case they will probably tell you what they think you want to hear. So you must then make sure you get confirmation of the answers they give you – *in writing* – and that the issues you've raised are covered in the contract. At this point, you again need the services of your independent *gestoria*/solicitor, as the contract will be in Spanish.

If you're renting rather than buying a property, you'll probably be dealing with a rental agent. Rental agents are covered later, under the section about property managers, but basically the same advice applies: don't trust them!

Buying to rent out as a holiday let

If you're looking at properties with a view to buying, the agents will probably tell you that there's tremendous holiday rental potential, and sometimes there is. However, sometimes there isn't. For example, there's hardly a square metre of building land remaining next to the sea on the Costas, so most new developments now tend to be slightly inland, and in some cases a couple of kilometres inland. There may be a bus service, but the chances are that it will be infrequent.

So, if you intend to rent out your new property when you're not using it yourself, *always* try to imagine you're a tourist before you make your purchase. *You* may not mind hiring a car for the duration of your visits in order to get around, but the chances are that this will not be something the average tourist wants to spend money on. So, if you're buying a property near the sea, you need to be as near to it as you can possibly get in order to generate a good holiday rental income.

Many people buy 'golf properties', which are apartments or houses built on complexes next to golf courses. They sound very grand, and people associate them with a certain amount of class and prestige. But be careful. The agent will tell you that these properties are in great demand from golfers for holiday lets, but that's only partly true, at best. When they come on holiday, most golfers want to play a different course every day, and certainly don't want to spend a week or a fortnight going round the same 19 holes. So, in reality, they're not going to pay a premium to rent a holiday apartment on a golf course.

The finder's fee
If you're looking to rent an apartment or villa long term (on an 11-month contract), you'll be lucky to get away without paying a finder's fee. Most property owners who want to rent out their apartment or villa will use a letting agent. You'll see a property advertised with a stated rent, contact the agent to enquire about it, and they'll show it to you. If you decide to take the property, you'll inevitably be asked to pay up front:

      1 month's deposit (at least); sometimes 2
+   1 month's rent in advance
+   1 month's rent as a finder's fee

The finder's fee is also sometimes called a management fee, and is payable only once on each let, at the outset prior to moving in. Do not make the same assumption I did. We rented a villa on the road up to Mijas village and were there for nearly two years. At the end of the first 11-month contract, we spoke to the agent and informed him that we would like to stay for a further 11 months.

'Fine,' said the agent. 'I will draw up another contract for signature.'

Very stupidly, I said, 'So that will be the first month's rent up front again, plus the management fee?'

'Yes, that's right,' said the agent.

We paid the money and spent another happy 11 months in our villa before moving on. Strange as it may sound, it wasn't until eight or nine months later that I discovered I shouldn't have paid the management fee again. It was my own stupid fault, as it was me who put the words into his mouth, and of course he wasn't going to argue. 'An extra 1,500 euros; thank you very much.'

As often as not, when you decide to leave the property you've rented, you won't get the deposit back. They'll make up any excuse, such as, 'That paint wasn't scratched,' or 'That tile wasn't cracked when you moved in.' So you would do well to assume that you'll lose the deposit, and write it off over the 11 months of your contract. If you've been lucky enough to find an honourable agent and you do get it back, look on it as a bonus.

We had an honourable agent (I think) when we rented the apartment we lived in prior to buying. We initially paid the standard one month's rent in advance, one month's agent's/finder's fee, and two months' returnable deposit. (Spanish owners usually insist on two months' returnable deposit, whereas British owners will usually accept one month.) There were things we weren't completely happy about and some things we simply couldn't live with, so we repainted the whole apartment, bought some new light fittings and a few other things to make it a nice home.

One month prior to the end of our rental contract, I informed the agent that we were giving notice, and he said, 'Fine. I will inform the owner so that he can come down and check the place over and give you your deposit back.' He phoned me shortly afterwards and told me that the owner and his wife were coming down from northern Spain at the weekend, and when they arrived they were absolutely delighted with the condition of the place, as it was far better than it had been when we took over. They both looked me in the eye, shook my hand, and told us – in front of the agent – that they would send the deposit down within a couple of days.

A few days later, the agent knocked on our door looking a bit sheepish and informed us that the owner had phoned him and said that he wasn't going to return our deposit (which was 1,600 euros). He hadn't given a reason, but was adamant that he wasn't going to pay it back. I was furious. How could he and his wife have looked us straight in the eye and lied about it?

The next day, I contacted our *gestoria* and arranged for us to have a meeting, at which he told me, quite casually, that it isn't unusual for Spanish owners to refuse to repay the deposit. Apparently, the only thing we could do was send official legal letters, although, at the end of the day, we could only recover the money by taking the owner to court, which would not only take forever, but would also cost more than the value of our deposit.

To this day, I haven't got that money back and I realise in hindsight that what I should have done was refuse to move out unless and until he returned it. So be careful!

The tourists

We lived in a beautiful apartment in a place called Riviera del Sol, which is next to Calahonda, between Fuengirola and Marbella. Riviera is an extremely nice place and we were delighted with the apartment we found, so we signed up for the standard 11-month rental contract. There were about 30 apartments in this relatively new complex, and ours was at the end of the second of three floors. I prefer to go for an end apartment whenever possible, as it means there's only the chance of neighbour noise coming through the walls on one side. This was a complex where owners lived themselves, or used the apartments for their own holiday use, or, in a couple of cases, let them out on long-term contracts to people like ourselves.

We'd only been in the apartment for a few weeks when one morning, at about 2 o'clock, a riot seemed to have broken out around the pool, which was below our balcony. We looked out and there were five or six tourists, pissed out of their heads, diving in the pool, singing, and being sick behind the bushes. After a couple of nights of the same thing, I phoned the lady who owned our apartment and told her about the problem. 'Oh yes,' she said. 'The people who own number *whatever* decided to advertise it on the Internet for holiday lets.' So that was that, at least until the holidays were over.

Tourists came and went and, within a few months, other owners had decided to do the same thing in order to generate extra cash from their holiday investment. It was like a circus. Now, I don't have anything against tourists enjoying themselves – I used to be one myself – but when you live here, the last thing you want is that lot kicking off through the night when you've got to get up for work the next day.

It's very common for owners to let their apartments for holiday lets, so be aware of this whether you're looking to buy for your own use or to rent long term. It can make your life absolute hell, particularly during the summer months.

The dogs

When you're planning to rent or purchase a villa, whether large or small, depending on your budget, there's another thing you wouldn't normally think to look for in the UK. People over here who live in villas seem to have this hang-up about having to own one or more large dogs. You'll probably look at a villa during the day; the sun is shining, it has its own private garden, possibly a pool, and you'll have complete privacy, peace and tranquillity. What could be better? But visit the property again during the night. Do this for a few nights at different times and I can almost guarantee that as soon as you get out of your car, Alsatians, Rottweilers, Boxers, you name it, will explode into a thunderous roar and wake up the whole bloody street.

Also what you have to take into account is that Spaniards are not famous for being a nation of dog lovers like the Brits are. To most Spanish people, an animal is an animal is an animal. So, if you live in an apartment and there's a dog owner in one of the apartments near you, you're probably in for some serious trouble. They go out to work and think nothing at all about leaving the dog(s) alone, and then it's 'yap yap bloody yap' all day every day. It makes matters far worse when they leave the patio door open so that the dog can go outside and relieve itself. If you happen to live in the apartment directly below one of these doggy-loo balconies, you'll inevitably get all sorts of stuff dripping down onto your balcony. Fortunately, we live at the top, so we haven't suffered from the problem, but we know lots of people who have, and it's very unpleasant.

While on the subjects of pets, the following happened to some friends of ours who have two young children and who rented a brand new apartment in a brand new community. Many of the apartments had been bought by speculators, who rented them out on long-term lets, and although they were okay, they were towards the bottom end of the luxury bracket, so the rents were fairly cheap. Result: scuzzers. Our friends were woken up at dawn one morning wondering what the hell was happening and whether they'd somehow been transported in their sleep to a farmyard. It turned out that the ear-splitting noise that had woken them was a cockerel, which was being kept on the balcony by the Spanish couple who'd moved in to the apartment next door.

Once he realised he wasn't imagining it, my friend had a word with this new guy and got a load of abuse, so he had no option but to report him to the president of the residents' committee. As it happened – and this is far from unusual – El Presidente of the community lived in

Madrid and only ever used his apartment for family holidays in August. So he didn't give a toss about this cockerel waking everyone up at dawn every morning, and it took five months to get rid of it, by which time my friend was ready to throw himself off his balcony.

The dustbin men

This may sound completely ridiculous to you, but if you view a house or an apartment in Spain with a view to buying it, make a point of finding out where the dustbins are. Rather than each house or apartment building having its own dustbin(s), there are usually large community dustbins located at various points down the roads.

The dustbin men work nights over here, which is a perfectly sensible thing to do for a number of reasons. Obviously the weather is hot during the day, particularly in the summer months, so it's cooler for them to work at night, and also there's very little traffic during the night, so they can get around much more easily and quickly. However, I guess they don't like the idea of working while everyone else is tucked up snugly in bed, so when the bin men come calling at 3 o'clock in the morning, they make as much racket as possible.

So, if the house or apartment you're viewing is near any dustbins, forget it.

First-floor apartments

If you are looking to buy a brand new apartment, or even if you're thinking about buying one 'off plan', beware of the first-floor apartment. If the development you're interested in is going to be purely residential, then this warning is not applicable; but if there are going to be commercial units on the ground floor, then watch out! As often as not, the apartments in a building will be sold first, before the empty shells of commercial units on the ground floor. So there's no way of knowing what the commercial units are going to be. The estate agent and/or developer may tell you that the unit below your proposed new first-floor apartment is going to be a hairdresser or a real-estate office. But how do you know for certain? And even if it is true (which is highly unlikely), who's to say that the business will survive? The unit could be sold again and turned into a karaoke bar. It happens, lots and lots of times.

So don't buy or rent a first-floor apartment above a commercial unit. The chances are that somewhere down the line the place will be turned into Screwy Louis' karaoke bar, and you'll be in the market for, at the very least, a lifetime's supply of sleeping tablets.

Spanish or British?

You may not have any preconceived ideas about whether you'd prefer to live amongst Brits, Spaniards or a mixture of both, but different complexes attract different types of people. For example, if the property is on or near a golf course, you'll inevitably be amongst fellow golfers. There are urbanisations that are a complete cross-section of nationalities, including Dutch, Danish, German, British and Spanish, and then there are the predominantly British urbanisations. So, if you're not careful, it can be like living in a suburb of Manchester but with sunshine.

Personally, I prefer the Spanish complexes. I can honestly say that in all the time we've lived amongst them, we've experienced nothing but total friendliness. If you're nice and polite to them, they're nice and polite to you. As often as not, you'll find that a Spanish complex is virtually empty for most of the year, as they tend to use these homes purely as holiday homes, coming down from Madrid, Cordoba, Seville or wherever for the odd weekend or Bank Holiday.

But, if you're moving to the Spanish coast, beware of August. Most of Spain just about closes during August, and it seems like half the population descends on the Costas. So what was an empty complex fills overnight, and it's like living in a Spanish Butlins. They rise in the morning and sit round the pool just like anyone else. Then, around 2.00 p.m., it's as though a bomb has dropped and everyone disappears for two or three hours for their *siesta* – adults, kids, everyone. Then, around 5 or 6 o'clock, they reappear and stay up until 2 or 3 in the morning talking. Well, actually, the Spanish don't talk, they shout, but it's done without any intention of offence.

So, unless you have treble-glazing, the best thing to do during August is go on holiday yourself: book into a hotel, rent out your apartment to a friend who doesn't know any better, but get the hell out. Then, come the 1st September, the peace and tranquillity return for another 11 months.

Community charges

If you decide to rent, you'll find as often as not that the community charge is built into the rent. But this is not always the case. Ask before you commit yourself, as it can make a considerable difference to your monthly outlay.

If you're planning to purchase a property on an urbanisation, the community charge is one of the first things to enquire about. How much is it? What one-off (ad-hoc) costs can you be hit with (e.g. external painting of the apartment blocks)? And by what rate/percentage can it increase per annum?

The differences in community charges never cease to amaze me, and you'll generally find that living on a Spanish complex is considerably cheaper than living on a predominantly foreign complex in terms of the community charge. As an example, we currently have an *attico* (penthouse/top-floor apartment) on a predominantly Spanish complex overlooking the sea, with beautifully tended gardens, two swimming pools and a tennis court. At the time of writing, our community charge is 105 euros per month. However, we know a couple who bought a brand new two-bedroom apartment on a predominantly British complex of similar size a couple of kilometres inland, fairly near a golf course, and who were horrified to find, once they took the keys, that their community charge was 240 euros per month. Too late; they'd already bought it and hadn't asked the question first.

After paying these extortionate community charges for eighteen months or so, these people happened to be staying in their apartment at the same time as the people next door were staying in theirs. The apartment in question is an end apartment (at one end of a block) whereas his neighbours apartment is a middle one. He was astounded to be informed by his neighbours that their community charge was a hundred euros per month cheaper than his.

'What, how come?'

'I haven't got a clue' said the neighbour, 'but I'm not complaining'.

Now then! See if you can find any logic in this one, but first of all let me explain how community charges are normally allocated to apartments or houses within a community. It's quite simple really; you pay according to the square meterage (floor area) of your apartment or property which is fair enough. The larger property you have, the more you pay. In other words, if you own a three bedroom apartment it will usually occupy more square metres than a two bedroom apartment on the same complex (unless it's a penthouse which tend to be bigger) and you therefore pay a higher community charge.

When this guy did a bit more digging he found out that someone, presumably the developer, had allocated the community charges based on the square meterage of the 'outside walls'. Can you believe that? This guy, and numerous others who owned end apartments, were paying nearly twice as much community charge as other people owning inside apartments with the same (or virtually the same) floor area.

Der – I don't quite follow that one. What possible reason can there be for this? Let's just explore the possible avenues of this guy's logic –

1) He has the ability to walk on walls instead of floors and thinks everyone else can as well.
2) He actually lives in an inside apartment himself and fixed the community charges   accordingly.
3) He fancies himself as a physicist and tried to use Einstein's theory of relativity ($E=MC^2$) to   calculate the community fees but got it wrong. He put the '2' in the wrong place and came up with ($E=M^2C$), which of course gives you (Extortion=Square Metres Calculated).
4) He's incredibly silly.

I think its number 4.

Anyway, the owner is still trying to get the situation rectified as I write this book, and getting absolutely nowhere at all. Even if it is resolved in a fair and proper way (very unlikely), there is not a chance in hell that he will be able to claim the discrepancy retrospectively.

It's called being robbed through lack of logic!

Ask the right questions. It can be expensive and very unfair if you don't!

Accruing

You might assume that all the costs of the community's amenities – the upkeep of the gardens, swimming pool etc. – are included in your community charge. But you'd be wrong. Accruing is really a subsection of 'Community charges', and I'm actually going through this issue as I'm writing this book.

The outsides of the four small blocks that make up our complex are in desperate need of painting. Hardly any buildings in Spain have guttering, so when it rains, all the dirt and rubbish is washed down from the roof and then runs down the outside of the walls of the building. This then dries out, and over a period of time the whitewashed or light-coloured rendered walls get streaky and dirty. Our complex is painted white, so it obviously shows the dirt up more, and it's starting to look a little sad.

'When is the outside of the buildings going to be painted?' I asked El Presidente.

'Oh, I don't know. It will have to go to a vote again'.

'Again? What do you mean "again"?' I asked. 'Surely you accrue for painting in the community charge and just get it done every two or three years or as and when necessary?'

'No, we don't do that. It does look a bit shabby, doesn't it?'

'Okay, so what do we do then? I can't believe you haven't been accruing for it, but couldn't we just get a few prices in and split the cost between the number of apartments?'

'Oh, we've already taken a vote on that for the last two years. The problem is that 44 out of the 48 apartments are owned by Spanish people (*mostly from Cordoba, for some reason*) who only use them during the month of August. They are empty for the other 11 months.'

I obviously knew that, as it was one of the attractions of buying our apartment in the first place.

'You see,' he said, 'as they are not here, they are not really bothered about the appearance of the place as long as they can just come down for their annual holiday in August. Therefore, they won't pay for the repainting.'

What these people don't seem to realise is that it won't be long before the appearance will start to affect the resale value of these properties, if it hasn't done so already.

Check it out. Accruing for painting is very important!

Community politics

One major problem of living in an apartment on a private urbanization can be the politics. In all probability there will be El Presidente and his cronies, 'I want to be' El Presidente and his cronies, and then a few renegades who just want to disagree with anything and everything that is put forward at community meetings. When we first purchased our apartment on a complex which, as previously mentioned, is virtually all Spanish owned, my command of the Spanish language was – er – crap actually. As I was desperate for the outside of the community buildings to be painted I spoke to El Presidente and asked if he would vote on my behalf at the meeting for the work to be done. 'Yes, of course, no problem as I agree that the work is necessary'.

About a week later I was talking to Manolo the gardener who is a great guy and does a brilliant job cleaning the pools and generally looking after the place. He took me by complete surprise when he said to me on this day –
'Why did you vote at the recent meeting to have me sacked?'
'Pardon'.
'I have seen the minutes of the meeting (so had I but they were in Spanish and didn't have a clue what they were on about) and you voted to have me sacked'.
'No I didn't'.
'Yes you did, I saw the votes'.
The penny dropped. I had signed a piece of paper giving El Presidente the right to cast a vote on my behalf on the painting issue. What he had also done is use my vote for any other particular issue which he believed in without consulting me. It gets worse. He had also got *seven* other absent owners who lived around Spain to sign the same piece of paper for the paint issue and used these also to try and sack the nice gardener type bloke. He was using a block vote of nine to try and do whatever he wanted.
Beware the community politics!

The cold and damp
The build quality in Spain is nothing like that in the UK. Double-skin walls? No. To compound the problem, it's not uncommon to find that there's no damp-proof course, and pointing has apparently not yet been invented in Spain. If you look at new properties being built, you'll see holes all over the place in the brickwork, and no pointing at all. Once the outside walls are plastered and painted, they look marvellous, but the holes are invariably still there underneath. Combine all these issues, and you'll have damp in the winter. It is seriously difficult to find a Spanish property that does not suffer from damp, and it's often extreme.

Although it isn't always practical to do so, view properties whenever possible in the winter, preferably during or shortly after a rainstorm. During the winter months, many properties smell damp and have black patches all over the walls of at least one room. Many people sleep in these damp conditions, breathing in the inevitable spores, and consequently colds and flu and other winter ailments are just as prevalent in Spain as they are in the UK. There aren't many days or weeks in the year when it *does* rain on the Costas, but when it rains, it rains heavily, and once the damp sets in to the walls, it's there until the spring.

Feeling the cold while indoors is the one thing that Brits drastically underestimate in Spain. Of course, for most of the year the weather is fantastic, but during the winter, when a cold, wet spell arrives, you really do feel it more than you would in the UK, even though in reality it's considerably warmer. The house you left in the UK almost certainly had central heating, carpets and double-glazing. It could be minus 3 degrees outside, but as soon as you walked through your front door, you were warm and cosy. In Spain, you'll probably have no central heating, there'll be cold marble floor tiles instead of carpets, and if you do have double-glazing, it's likely to fit as well as a size 10 boot on a size 8 foot. Properties are primarily built to stay cool, not warm.

Many, if not most, of the new properties being built at present have reversible air conditioning. In other words, it can be used to cool a property in the summer and heat it during the winter. But most people put up with stand-alone electric or gas heaters. The electric heaters are quite expensive to run, so you'll find that most people use what is, in effect, a gas bottle in a tin box. These gas bottles are sold at most petrol stations, and you'll soon get used to trailing down the road to change your empty one. However – and it may just be me – I don't trust the gas-bottle heaters. They give off a distinct smell and induce in me visions of waking up dead one morning. So, personally, I'd rather pay the extra for electric heaters.

The best electric heaters we found were the plug-in, oil-filled radiators, but make sure you buy one with a built-in thermostat, which will cost slightly more. You can leave these on low during the day and they'll keep a room aired and, hopefully, limit the damp. Then, when you get home, you can fire them up onto full.

There's another alternative: a proper fire. Most Spanish properties are built with a real chimney in the lounge, but be careful. Unless you're in your sixties or seventies and remember the skills required for lighting a real fire from your childhood, you'll probably set light to your home, as I nearly did when we lived in our rented villa.

'This will be great,' I thought. 'I'll buy some logs from the petrol station (I can have a pint while I'm in there – yes, lads, it's not only the bakers that sell beer) and use a few old newspapers to get it going.

We'll not only be warm, but it will be quite romantic as well, won't it?'
Well, no, not unless you've bought an asbestos hat first.

I gathered together my logs, old newspapers, a few twigs from outside, and lit the fire. But why was all the smoke coming back into the lounge? Chris suggested I look up the chimney, which isn't easy when six old copies of a newspaper are burning like an inferno. Then the smoke alarm went off. 'Quick! Don't panic! I'll just pull the paper and logs out of the fire. Have you got a stick or something, because there's no way I'm putting my hand in there?' As I'm shouting all this, I'm running around the lounge like a mad dog. 'Quick! Whack the bloody smoke alarm 'cos it's doing my head in.'

'I would,' Chris said, trying not to let her rising panic show, 'but I can't see it. In fact, I can't see you either.'

This was getting serious, so I legged it into the kitchen, picked up a pan, filled it with water and chucked it into the fire. Back to the kitchen for a refill, and by this time the room was seriously full of smoke. More water. We opened all the doors and windows and from the outside it must have looked as though we were electing a new Pope. There was nothing for it but to sit outside with blackened faces and let the smoke clear.

When we went back in, an hour or so later, we could have cried. Apparently I'd missed with one of the pans full of water and thrown it all over our DVD player, and the new cream coloured rug Chris had recently purchased looked as if it had been dragged across the local sewage works.

I was ashamed; I was in the Boy Scouts, you know.

One final word on the subject of damp in Spanish properties, which may sound trivial but is something you ignore at your peril – silicone. The first time it rains heavily after you've moved in to your new Spanish home, whether rented or bought, you'll think you're living in a huge concrete colander. There'll be water spouting in from every orifice – both the ones you already knew you had and ones you never even imagined existed. You'll have drips, trickles, streams and, if you're really unlucky, bloody great waterfalls. What you need is a pump pack or ten of silicone – it's possibly the most useful purchase you'll ever make – and, if death by drowning doesn't appeal to you, pump it diligently into every crack and joint.

The hot-water boiler

It may seem a trivial thing to mention if you're in the process of buying a brand new house or apartment, but asking the question 'What is the capacity of the hot-water boiler?' can save you a substantial amount of money.

Many developers fit 20-litre hot-water boilers into new properties for two simple reasons: (a) they're cheaper to buy, and (b) they fit inside standard kitchen wall units. But they're next to useless: you'll be lucky to get a brief shower out of a boiler with a 20-litre capacity. You need at least 80 litres or, preferably, 100 litres. Replacing the boiler could cost you around 2000 euros, because unless you're prepared to rip out half your brand new kitchen, it will have to go in an adjoining bedroom or a bathroom, which will involve having to pay for new pipe work, plastering, re-tiling, the new boiler itself and labour.

Unless there's something in the contract stating the capacity of the hot-water boiler, in all likelihood you'll get the 20 litre. Arguing that it isn't 'fit for purpose' once the keys of the property have been handed over to you will be a waste of time. So do remember to ask this question before you sign the contract.

The community underground car park

If you buy or rent a villa or townhouse in Spain, you're likely to get a private, individual garage for your vehicle. Many houses are built in such a way that these garages are beneath the property, and in many cases they're huge, like aircraft hangers. People will often take advantage of this additional space and create an extra room for the children, a bar, pool room or whatever. If, on the other hand, you buy or rent an apartment, you'll get either road parking or your own numbered bay within the community underground car park, which will probably be secure from outsiders, with access via electric gates.

Beware. Many vendettas in Spain are conducted in the community underground car park. They might have started because of noise from a stereo, slamming doors during the night, stiletto heels from the apartment above, scraping furniture on the floor, a barking dog, anything. But if you speak to Brits who have lived in Spain for a number of years, you'll struggle to find one who hasn't had their own vehicle damaged within the community underground car park or knows someone who has.

The favourite activity is sticking a knife through one or all of your tyres. This happened to my Harley Davidson, and I still don't know to this day why or by whom. Also, a friend of Chris's son bought a gleaming, bright red 3 Series BMW, which, understandably, he was chuffed to bits with. Only two days later, he went down to the community underground car park and someone had poured a full can of paint stripper all over the bonnet.

Although these places are usually secure from outsiders, they are not secure from other people who live or stay on the complex, and, as with virtually anywhere else, there are some very nasty people down here.

One further note of caution in relation to these car parks: some have one large garage door for both entry and exit, but many have two doors, one for entry and the other for exit. These are usually huge electronic doors that are opened with a 'zapper'. Beware of the apartment directly over the top of these entry and exit doors. Throughout the night, these bloody great things bang open and closed, making it virtually impossible to get a decent night's sleep. Avoid these apartments like the plague.

Who pays for the repairs in rented property?
If you rent a property from a Spaniard and something breaks, it's likely to be *you*, not the owner, who's expected to pay for repairing it. In the UK, things are generally the other way around. For instance, if the water heater packs in and you phone your agent to inform him of the fact, the reply you'll usually get will be, 'Then fix it.' It may be that the washing machine has broken down, 'Then fix it.' It's a shock. You don't expect that; you assume the owner will sort it out. But he won't. However, the agent may respond with a helpful, 'My brother is a heating engineer,' or 'I can get someone out quickly.' Read into it what you will.

The 'snagging list'
When you buy a brand new property and finally get the key, which will probably be considerably later than agreed, you'll be asked to spend a little time there and have a good look round. Try the appliances, check the fit of the doors, make sure the loos flush, and generally make sure everything is to your satisfaction. Take this to the extreme. Rev everything up to breaking point, turn it off, and then rev it up again. Make absolutely certain that everything is in full working order, because if you don't, trying to get things fixed afterwards will be more or less a non-starter.

You'll be very fortunate if you don't find anything that requires attention. So, once you've discovered the faults and generated your snagging list, how do you get the jobs done? You'll probably be in the UK, and many developers will not hold your keys once they've been handed over to you – they don't want to take responsibility if someone goes in there. So how do the workmen get in? These outstanding jobs can take months to sort out, and I've known people who've been literally tearing their hair out not knowing where to turn next, and have got so frustrated they've sold the bloody thing before they even had one holiday in it.

This is not the UK, and, as I've mentioned before, customer service has not yet been invented in most Spanish businesses. As an example, I highlight below the experience of a couple of friends of mine. I'm not saying this is the norm, but it's certainly not unusual.

The couple in question are keen golfers who live in the UK and bought a brand new, two-bedroom, two-bathroom apartment near the Torrequebrada Golf Course. They became so frustrated being in the UK and not able to get any sense or action from the developer that they asked for our help. We agreed to hold a key for them and to try to get the outstanding jobs done from this end, letting in the workmen, if and when they arrived, and being present while work was being carried out.

They'd bought the property 'off-plan', as many people do, and it was due to be completed during March, although they didn't actually get the keys until the end of October. They then visited the apartment in mid-November in order to compile the snagging list, which is when a whole new nightmare began. Chris and I were constantly making telephone calls to the developer, as were the owners from the UK. Eventually, during February, almost a year after the original completion date, having realised they weren't making any progress whatsoever, they contacted the real-estate company through which they'd made the purchase. They sent an e-mail to the sales manager listing all the problems they'd had and all the money they'd been forced to spend on alternative accommodation for the holidays they'd booked having been assured that everything was in order, only to arrive and find that the apartment still wasn't habitable.

Someone at a very high level within the real-estate company obviously spoke to a director at the developers. I received a call only a few days later, asking if I could be at the apartment the following afternoon in order for someone to view the problems and rectify them. Great. Things are going to get fixed. Wrong.

As agreed, I arrived the following afternoon and Maria, our contact at the developers, turned up with two guys wearing black designer suits, shiny shoes and sunglasses and looking like The Blues Brothers. Maria explained that they were actually directors of the development company and wanted to see for themselves what all the fuss was about.

'Hang on a minute, Maria. You mean these guys are only looking? The jobs are not actually going to be done today?'

'Well, possibly. If they can fix anything themselves, they will,' she told me.

In Armani suits and sunglasses? I don't think so.

The next thing I knew, these guys were standing on dining-room chairs. One was poking around in the air vents for the air-con, and the other was trying to prise the microwave out of its housing using a pen. I lent them a VW screwdriver out of the toolkit in my car, and they forced the air-con vent off the ceiling in each bedroom. Apparently there's a fin inside that was in the wrong position, not allowing air into the rooms. Fine. One job done.

They agreed about the existence of the other problems and then suited and booted, they left. Maria told me that they'd now have to pay someone to come and rectify the faults at a later date and that the developers would get their own technician to look at the electric shutter and microwave. A new boiler was also required, but it would be virtually impossible to get the company who installed it to return, so they'd take one out of another apartment that hadn't yet been sold. Presumably at some point down the line, the poor sods who eventually bought this other apartment would have to go through the same procedure of chasing a new boiler.

Sure enough, after making a number of calls to their office, I was eventually asked to be at the property again one afternoon. I waited for their 'technician', who arrived with another member of the sales staff I'd spoken to on the phone, who we'll call Marco. The technician looked at the microwave and confirmed that there was no electricity going into it; but this wasn't something he could do himself. He then dismantled the electric window shutter in the lounge with a large penknife, and showed me the badly bent girder around which the shutter winds. He described it as a girder because it was load bearing, but in fact it was only made out of aluminium, and didn't look as if it would take the weight of a dead hamster. 'It requires a new girder, which will have to be ordered from the manufacturer,' he said. Luckily, the shutter in the other bedroom was a two-minute job, changing the wires around in the switch. So not a terrific amount of progress there then.

Marco told me that Spain is completely different from the UK, as most jobs are subcontracted. Once they're complete, the subcontractors disappear and it's virtually impossible to get them back to rectify any problems.

'So why don't you hold monies back as security until they've repaired the faults?' I asked him.

'Oh we do, 5%. But all they do is build the 5% into their price at the outset and then walk away. They're not interested.'

'But surely that gives them a bad reputation and they don't get any more work from you?'

'No. They all do it, so they are all as bad as each other'.

'So what about customer service after sales? It doesn't exist.'

'I know,' he said. 'It's terrible isn't it? But this is Spain and things take much longer here.'

After more telephone calls and two more visits, the jobs were all done. But if my friend had tried to do it alone from the UK, he wouldn't have stood a chance.

So beware of these issues. Think everything through and take your time. If you're going to invest your hard-earned money in brand new Spanish property, it's vital to know what you might be letting yourself in for. The telephone is a fob-off accessory, and I've known people who've spent not hundreds, but thousands of pounds on flights over here in order to try to get things done face to face. And even when they do come over, the workmen invariably don't turn up, or a new part is required from the manufacturer – and the game starts again. Also, if the problems are serious enough for you to be unable to stay in your own apartment, you'll have the extra cost of accommodation. It's expensive and it's frustrating and, in extreme cases, what started off as a dream becomes a nightmarish liability.

Hundreds of thousands of British people have already bought properties in Spain, and many hundreds of thousands more will do so in the coming years, and I'm sure that, for some of them at least, the process has been no more stressful than it would have been in the UK. But it's important to be aware of the different issues you'll encounter here, and to be prepared for the things that can go wrong, particularly if you're buying 'off-plan'.

Chapter 11
Some of the pitfalls of buying property in Spain

There are two popular sayings related to the purchase of property over here.

1) If there's any spare land around it, you can almost guarantee it will be built on. In other words, if you have a view now, the chances are that you won't have it for long.
2) If you can't touch it and see it, don't buy it – off plan!

Property prices doubled in Spain in just five years, and it's the only country in Europe where the value of property increased at a greater rate than in the UK – where prices rose by about 90% in the same period. But the average house price in Spain as a whole is still lower than in the UK and there are bargains available if you take the time to look around and do your research properly. The mass influx of Brits, as well as people from other European countries, who are buying holiday or retirement homes here means that there are rich pickings for cynical and unscrupulous property developers, and plenty of scams to catch out the unwary.

Property developers do it for the money
A very good friend of ours bought a brand new town house in Los Pacos, which is just on the outskirts of Fuengirola. He bought the end one of six, which has four bedrooms, an enormous underground garage and a shared pool. The house is in an elevated position on a hillside and the view from his front terrace was magnificent. The sea is about a mile away and you could see Fuengirola promenade, as well as all the boats. He was, quite rightly, very proud of his new house, and particularly of the fantastic views, and would sit on his terrace in the

evening with a glass of wine or a beer and look at the lights of Fuengirola in the distance.

Then, once all the houses in the row were finished and sold, the builder moved his equipment onto the land right in front of the terrace. Foundations were dug out and walls began to appear – 'That wasn't on the plans when I looked at them.' Before too long, a wall was completely blocking his view and it quickly became evident that the builder was building another row of town houses directly in front of his and at right angles to it. In other words, the spectacular views to the sea from his terrace and lounge have been replaced by a view of the gable end of another house – and that's quite literally all he can see now.

There's an area between Fuengirola and La Cala where a particular Spanish family own a row of seven small bungalows, all side by side. The bungalows are predominantly occupied by family members – the mother, son number one and family, son number two and family, daughter and family etc. – with a couple of them being rented out on long-term contracts. There was an area of elevated spare land behind the houses, which the family also owned and which they sold to a developer for the construction of a number of very large, very expensive semi-detached villas.

Prior to the land sale, the family secured planning permission to put another floor on some or all of the original bungalows – and then did nothing. The developer moved in and proceeded to build the new, very nice, properties behind the bungalows, and they were all sold very quickly off-plan. Of course, the people who bought these new houses didn't have a clue that planning permission had been given to the bungalows directly in front of them. As I write, the houses are almost ready for occupation and no move has yet been made to extend any of the existing bungalows. They'll wait until all the monies have been paid and the new purchasers have moved in. Then, before you can say 'nice outlook', work will commence – in effect blocking a good part of the view directly in front of the new houses. There's absolutely nothing these people will be able to do about it, as planning permission was already in place prior to the construction of their properties.

It's cynical, it's nasty, and it's premeditated. But, unfortunately, it's also not unusual, and the developers don't give a damn.

Golf properties sell for a premium, for obvious reasons – they're next to a golf course, and sometimes look out over one of the greens. Now that's got snob value, hasn't it? If you buy a villa or apartment on one of these developments, you pay a large premium for what's called 'front line'; in other words, uninterrupted views over the golf course. Normally, on the original plans, these properties are shown (and built) quite a distance from the course itself – you don't want a golf ball through your front window, do you? Of course not. But once the front-line properties are built and sold, you'll often see another row of villas or apartments going up in front of the front line – and the front line has suddenly become the second line. Sometimes this will happen again, and your premium front-line property is now three lines removed from the golf course, and your 'impressive view' is now the back of other houses or apartments. That really is a dirty trick, but believe me, it happens. Who knows, at some point some developer will probably build over the whole golf course once all the properties have been sold!

Mañana doesn't always mean tomorrow

At one point, Chris and I were developer victims too, indirectly, when we bought our apartment and became involved in a Spanish nightmare. It's so easily done. You don't see it coming because you don't know what you should be looking for. They say in the UK that moving or buying a house is second only to divorce in terms of stress and pressure. I'd suggest that moving or buying a property in Spain can be way beyond any divorce pressure you can imagine.

We first looked at our apartment in June 2004. It's a two-bedroom, two-bathroom, penthouse/*attico* (posh names for a top-floor flat), with a frontal sea view, which is in your face when you open the curtains in the morning. From the balcony, there's a spiral staircase going up to the roof garden, which covers the full area of the apartment. The views are stunning. At one side is fresh air and on the other side is the stairwell, so there's no chance of neighbour TV or hi-fi noise – and that's difficult to find, very difficult indeed.

We immediately fell in love with it, and, having spent four years looking, were convinced that this was definitely the one for us. We'd heard through a friend of ours that the Spanish owners were selling, but there was no 'For sale' sign in evidence. When we spoke to them, they explained that they were having a house built and that it would not be complete until December, so they were not actually looking to sell just yet. So, as we really wanted this property, we agreed to talk again in September.

Sure enough, when September arrived, we went to see them again and had another look around just to make sure. Yes, we still definitely wanted it. The jousting began over price, but there was no way these people would budge an inch. They wouldn't drop 1 euro, and as we didn't want them to put it on the market, we agreed to pay the full asking price. It hurt, but during the last three years of looking, albeit casually, we'd seen every kind of property you can imagine, and this one had everything we wanted, and more.

The house these people were having built was behind schedule (what a surprise!) and, rather than a December completion, they were now looking at January or February at the very latest – honest. They wanted to leave the completion date open, but, knowing Spanish builders as we did, there was no way we were going to agree to that. So, although we weren't happy about it, we reluctantly consented to completion on 31st March. This gave them a month's buffer over and above the end of February – which was, they assured us, the very, very, very latest completion date given by the builders.

We met at our *gestoria*'s office, signed the contract and handed over the standard 10% deposit. Then we began looking at new furniture, patio furniture, light fittings and all the other things we'd want when we moved in. Meanwhile, the end of March loomed.

Around mid-February, the guy we were buying our apartment from contacted us and asked for a meeting. Initially when we turned up at a café he'd suggested, he just danced around the subject we knew he was going to raise. But it had to come, and it did.

'Our house is still behind schedule and we would like to change the contract again. We want to move the completion date back seven, eight or possibly nine weeks.'

Is he taking the piss, or do the Spanish celebrate April Fools' Day in February? No, he was deadly serious. Chris and I looked at each other – no, no, no. But he insisted we should have a meeting at the office of our *gestoria* as soon as possible, and we agreed because this had to be sorted.

A couple of nights later, there we were again, and our *gestoria* was great. The guy we were buying from and his wife got very over-excited, but I could only follow some of the conversation, because once the Spanish 'go off on one', they speak so quickly that it's impossible even to detect the breaks between words. Chris and I just sighed and looked out of the window, until eventually, our *gestoria* spoke.

'These people are refusing to leave at the end of March as stated in the contract signed by both parties. They insist on an extension of up to three months. I have told them that if they will not move on this, and if you do not agree, they are in breach of the contract, therefore owing to you *double* the deposit you paid them.'

In Spain, if a seller takes a deposit from a purchaser and then breaks the contract, they have to pay the purchaser double the deposit amount. But these people called the bluff. They wouldn't move on anything; so we danced around again, trying to find a compromise.

There were all kinds of things to consider, not least the fact that we'd already given a month's notice on our rented apartment. There was also the mortgage – how long would the bank hold it for? We agreed to meet again the following evening after Chris and I had discussed it further and our *gestoria* had spoken to the bank regarding our mortgage.

The next night, off they go again, shouting, waving their arms around and banging papers down on the desk. Chris and I just crossed our legs, folded our arms, and again gazed out through the window. Just let them get on with it. If this had taken place in the UK, you can imagine one of the blokes just standing up and slotting the other one. Job done. Finally, our *gestoria* spoke again.

'The best compromise I can agree on is for the completion contract to be changed to the end of May, two months. These people will not get any more money until that point. Then the keys MUST be handed over, as the mortgage will have gone through and the property will be owned by you.'

It was not what Chris and I were looking for, but we really wanted this apartment and were not prepared to lose it for the sake of having to wait two months. Okay, we could dig our heels in and they'd have to pay us back double our deposit, but in the greater scheme of things that wasn't a fortune. It would mean that it would be 11 months from the first time we viewed the place to moving in, but what the hell, we'd wait.

Sometimes you have to take a deep breath and back off. Being stubborn can make you feel better initially, but it can cost you in the long run.

All because a developer was late – again.

Buying a property over here often involves 'black money', as it does when buying a business, but for different reasons. If you find a property you want to purchase for, say, 300,000 euros, it may go through as a sale for, say, 220,000 euros for tax reasons. That means that the transaction will go through at 220,000 euros and you'll get the old briefcase out again. You'll fill it with 80,000 euros in cash, put a baseball bat down your trouser leg just in case, and then deliver it to the seller (the money, that is). Then, if and when you come to sell the property, you may go through exactly the same process, but this time you could be on the receiving end of the brief case full of money.

You might want to employ a property manager – and then again, you might not

Once you've managed to manoeuvre your way around all the pitfalls, scams and delays, and you've bought your dream property in Spain, you might want to think about employing a property manager.

The majority of British-owned properties on the Costa del Sol are unoccupied for most of the year. Some owners rent them out on long-term (11-month) contracts to people who live here. Others rent them out as holiday lets, on the Internet, through agents, in the newspaper, or in other ways. Most use their properties for their own holiday use and occasionally for family and close friends – and many of these people employ property managers.

There are lots and lots of property management companies, and some of them are excellent. But there are also some really bad ones, with unscrupulous people playing tricks you'd find difficult to believe. Many of the large real-estate companies offer property management services, and there are also hundreds of small private property managers who invariably start off with a couple of properties and then expand into a decent-sized business.

The role of property managers is to look after your investment while you're in the UK. They'll visit the property to make sure everything's in order; clean it prior to visitors arriving and after they've left; sometimes offer to provide pre-visit shopping; and will be there in case someone locks themselves out or breaks something. If you use the right people, property managers are great assets, and you can feel comfortable that your investment is safe in your absence. But if someone holds a key to your property, it's imperative that you can trust them 100% - and that's not easy.

First of all, we'll consider the large real-estate companies.

Let's just say you bought your property through 'James' at one of the major real-estate companies on the coast. You've been delighted with the service you received from James, so when he offers you the company's property management service, the trust factor is already there. You go with them – why not? The problem is that it will not be James personally who visits and cleans your apartment; it will be someone else, probably a subcontracted cleaner, who actually does the work. That's a key in another set of hands. For all you know – and it happens – the cleaner is letting his or her relatives or friends stay in your property when it's empty. You wouldn't know, would you? How could you?

Then there are the small, independent property management companies. If you go with one of these, they'll have to hold a key. As in the UK, you can go into one of many shops in Spain and get a key cut in minutes. You'd be absolutely horrified if you knew how many apartments, town houses and villas are lived in at some point without the owner in the UK having a clue what's going on. People with access to property keys may be letting their friends, parents, children or whoever stay in YOUR apartment, free of charge. Sometimes they'll actually charge for the privilege, and could be making good money out of YOUR investment.

We knew an Irish lady who had an apartment in Calahonda. She'd used a local property management company and, to the best of her knowledge, everything was going fine. During one of her many visits she happened to mention to her property managers that her apartment insurance was due for payment. She would have to renew it while she was over. 'Oh, don't you bother with that,' they told her. 'Leave the money with us and we'll sort it out for you. We get much better rates. It's all part of the service.'

A few weeks passed, and she received a call in Ireland from one of her neighbours in Calahonda, who informed her that the people in the apartment above hers had left a bath running and completely flooded her premises. This lady jumped on a plane and was horrified to see the mess when she arrived: lounge suite, beds, everything ruined. She then proceeded to the property managers and explained about the mess, which they were not even aware of – obviously they hadn't been anywhere near her apartment for some time, despite that being precisely what they were being paid to do.

'Well, at least I'm insured.'

'Err, well, no actually. We never paid the premium.'

These are the kind of people some owners are dealing with. So always go with a recommendation from another owner who has had consistently good service, for a reasonable amount of time, from a property manager. If you have any suspicion whatsoever that a key may be in the hands of someone else, change the lock immediately. It's not expensive, and the small investment could save you a fortune.

It's also always a good idea to make friends with people in neighbouring properties. However, this isn't always easy, as you may only be staying in your property two, three of maybe four times a year. But the more people you get talking to, the better. You needn't be best friends with them, but at least if you've had a conversation or two, they'll probably keep an eye on your property while they are there and you are not.

It works both ways: make the suggestion to them that you reciprocate the arrangement. Even suggest that they put a short note under your door while you're away, informing you of any visitors. And swap telephone numbers. It's in everyone's interest at the end of the day, and if you can help each other to avoid the non-paying guest, so much the better. This is not being a nosey neighbour; it's just common sense, and well worth doing.

The worst-case scenario resulting from your key being in the wrong hands is 'the clear out' – it's certainly not a common occurrence, but it does happen. Your key is lent to someone, possibly a subcontract cleaner or workman, who nips down to the local hardware store and gets a key cut. A few days later, or possibly a few weeks later, that person pulls up with a van and clears the property out – furniture, TV, DVD player, the lot. The first you're likely to know about this is when you next visit. What are you going to be able to sort out in a week or two? Not a lot – but it'll certainly ruin your holiday.

Of course, you can take all the precautions available to you and still be the victim of plain bad luck. Two people we knew bought a first-floor apartment many years ago in the Dona Sofia complex at the west side of Fuengirola. Having purchased the property, they returned to the UK with a view to moving over here permanently at some point in the fairly near future. Three weeks after returning to the UK, this guy was having a haircut in his local barber's shop when over the radio came the news that 'a bomb has gone off in Fuengirola'. He turned to the barber and said, 'Ha ha, knowing my bloody luck, that bomb will have gone off right outside my new apartment.'

The next morning, he bought a newspaper and there it was – a view of the front of his pride-and-joy apartment with the shit blown out of it. The bomb had gone off outside Las Piramides Hotel, which just happened to be exactly opposite his new apartment. He was insured, but it took him forever to get the money out of the insurance company and rectify what looked like a scene from a war zone. If he'd walked into a bookie's office the day before the bomb had totalled his new apartment, what odds could he have got against that happening?

It was bad luck, pure and simple, and there's nothing you can do to avoid it. But you do need to think carefully about the ways in which you *are* able to protect your investment in Spain, and even if you're not normally of a suspicious nature, be careful who you trust.

Talking of which… An acquaintance of mine down here on the Costa del Sol who makes a living out of doing DIY jobs told me his story one evening over a few beers. I'd only known him for a few months, and didn't know a great deal about him other than the fact that he'd split up from his wife somewhere in Norfolk three years previously, come over for a holiday and never gone back. We got talking on this particular evening and I commented that it must be difficult for him when he doesn't have any work for a week or so.

'Very difficult,' he said. 'This wasn't the idea originally, but a so-called friend I met over here stole £35,000 off me, which was the only money I had in the whole world.'

'How the hell did he manage to do that?' I asked.

'I trusted him and I shouldn't have; simple as that,' he answered, and then told me his story.

Mike – not his real name – came over here and got friendly with a guy and his wife who were from the same part of the world, and once Mike decided not to go back to the UK, he and this guy – who worked at a real-estate company – became even closer. During their many conversations about the real-estate market, this guy kept telling Mike that you could still buy village properties inland for about £60,000, but that this wouldn't be the case for very long. Stupidly, Mike had already mentioned his £35,000, and over a period of time the real-estate guy convinced him that they should buy a village property and renovate it. The idea was that Mike would do the renovation, as he's extremely good at anything involving building, plumbing, electrics etc.

'We'll each put in half the money,' the guy told him. 'Then you do the renovation and when we sell, you'll be paid for the work you've done and we'll split the rest of the proceeds. Of course, to make it simpler and quicker, we'll have to buy the property in my name, because you're not an official resident.'

And Mike went for it – after all, the guy was his mate, and a really nice man.

So they bought a house in a village up in the Granada hills, renovated it and then put it on the market, and Mike was convinced that he was going to make a very tidy profit, as he'd managed to transform the house into a perfect holiday home for any northern European couple.

By this time, Mike had moved further along the coast to Fuengirola, as most of his work was coming from that area, and he was finding that the real-estate guy had become a bit elusive. Then, after a while, his friend's mobile number suddenly became 'unobtainable' and, starting to feel a little anxious, Mike eventually set out to track him down, only to find that he'd disappeared without a trace. The house had been sold and Mike's 'friend' had legged it with all the money, including Mike's £35,000 investment – and was never seen again.

Many of the people who will try to rob you in Spain are Brits, and they get away with it simply because they play on the friendly 'trust me' factor. But they're not the only ones.

I know a family who bought a very nice four-storey town house just outside Fuengirola, at one end of a block of three. They paid cash, were handed the keys, and moved in fairly quickly. New builds are piped in to what's called "builders' electric" until the electricity company come and fit proper meters once the whole project is complete, and this guy Shaun's house was no exception. Sometimes it can take three or four months from completion until the electricity company get around to installing a meter, so it's free electricity up until that point in time.

One day, after these people had been living in their new house for nearly six months, the electricity went off without warning. The Scandinavian family who owned the other end house only used it for holidays, but Shaun checked with the Spanish family next door and their electricity was off also, which was fortunate because Shaun didn't speak much Spanish and he was able to rely on the Spanish guy to help sort out the problem with the relevant people at the Town Hall and the electricity company.

It turned out that what had happened was this: the developer hadn't been supplied with builders' electricity, and wasn't paying for it, but he had hacked into the street supply. So when the electricity company came to fit the meters and discovered what had been done, they immediately cut the electricity supply to the three new houses. Meanwhile, the developer had disappeared from the face of the earth and couldn't be traced. So Shaun – who has a wife and two young children – had no option but to rent an apartment at 1,000 euros a month until the problem was sorted out.

But worse was to come, as the electricity company wouldn't fit the meters until the electricity that had been used prior to disconnection was paid for, but this couldn't be done because nobody could trace the developer. Shaun, the Spanish family and the Scandinavian family offered to split the cost and pay it themselves to get the supply back on, but they couldn't do that either, because it then transpired that the houses hadn't been granted an occupancy licence – largely because the developer had never applied for one.

Five months passed and the three families were tearing their hair out and getting desperate, until finally the council came to inspect the properties with a view to granting the occupancy licence and then enabling the meters to be installed. But once the council inspector arrived, he found all kinds of things that were not to specification, not least the fact that the pavement running around three sides of the development was the wrong height and would have to be ripped up and remade. The three families had no option but to get all the work done at their own expense, and they finally moved back into their houses after 15 months, having had to foot the bill for all the building work and, in Shaun's case, having spent 15,000 euros on renting an apartment because they couldn't live in their own home. Fortunately they had the money to finance it all, but if they hadn't, it would probably have led them to financial meltdown.

I can't emphasise it often enough: check everything – and trust no one!

Repossession

Something happened to a friend of mine recently that I have to tell you about before we move on. It's so wacky that you'll probably have serious trouble believing it. It is true though, I can assure you.

Unfortunately, this friend of mine who lives in the UK has found himself in financial meltdown and is in the process of having his holiday home here in Mijas Costa repossessed by the bank (a Spanish bank). This very nice two bedroom/2 bathroom apartment is in the Miraflores area and when he bought it he took the option and paid extra for a car parking space and a lock up store room. Due to his unfortunate predicament, he has fallen well behind with his mortgage payments and the bank informed him recently that they were repossessing by the end of February. He has no alternative but to accept this and saw it coming, but what he didn't expect was the bank saying that they were taking his apartment but didn't want the car parking space or the store room.

'What? But they're no good to me and were part of the original purchase package'.

'No, we don't want them; you will have to keep them'.

'But you can have them for free. What good to me are a car parking space and a lock up store room in a complex where I don't even have an apartment'?

'Sorry, not our problem and we don't want them'.

Are they barking mad? Surely when they auction this property, as they surely will in order to pull back as much capital as they can from it, they would get more for it or at least make it more saleable if it included a parking space and a store room – wouldn't they?

What on earth is this guy going to do with them? Does he still have to pay 'part' community charges forever and a day just for a parking space and a store room?

Is it just me – what are they on?

Chapter 12
Finding a 'proper' job

People who move to Spain without the financial resources to buy a business of their own will face the task of finding a job. It isn't too difficult to find something casual or part time, but finding a 'proper' job is very difficult indeed. It isn't easy to come down here and earn a decent living, not easy at all – and that's something you need to understand before you make the move.

Generally speaking, cleaning and babysitting pay more than bar work, but these jobs are difficult to find, as most are already filled with people who have been here a while and know the ropes. As far as cleaning is concerned, there are two main options. You can either work for a British property agent cleaning holiday let properties or secure cleaning jobs at private properties owned by people who live here permanently. If you take the first option, you will almost certainly be cleaning apartments within a fairly small area, and therefore no travel is involved. However, if you go for the second option, you'll have to build up a list of private clients yourself, and that will inevitably require transport, as well as unpaid time spent travelling. Either way, you can expect to earn double per hour what you'd earn working in most bars or restaurants. But these cleaning jobs are very difficult to secure (for a decent rate of pay).

With regard to babysitting, this can pay very well indeed in Spain, but you will have had to live here for a significant amount of time before anyone will even consider using you. People don't allow total strangers into their homes to look after their children unless they've been very highly recommended by a friend. However, women who get over that hurdle can earn good money, as there are some very wealthy people here who will pay handsomely for a good, reliable, trustworthy babysitter.

Wages in Spain are nowhere near what they are in the UK. For instance, if you can get a job in a bar or restaurant, you'll be looking at being paid around 5 or 6 euros per hour. You wouldn't get out of bed for that in the UK. I've known people who've taken bar jobs out of desperation at 3 euros per hour. Can you live on that? I doubt it. Not even out here.

If you do secure a job, it's very difficult to find an employer who is willing to put you on a proper employment contract. Having a contract involves the cost to an employer of National Insurance, and small businesses are rarely prepared to pay this. Then there is the cost of holiday pay and sick pay. Employees also have far more employment rights in Spain, so it's very difficult and expensive to 'get rid' of someone, particularly if they're on a full-time contract.

As the Costas are geared to tourism and property development, it stands to reason that many of the jobs that are on offer are within these sectors. In the UK, if you pick up a local newspaper and look at the situations vacant section, there will probably be a wide range of jobs for secretaries, motor mechanics, local government officers, printers, electricians, plumbers, you name it. If you look at one of the local Costa del Sol English language newspapers, however, you'll see a different story completely. Most advertised positions are for telesales staff (commission based), real-estate sales staff (commission based), timeshare sales staff (commission based) and bar work (around 5 euros per hour) – that's it. The commission-based jobs are 'jam tomorrow' jobs. How can you budget your living costs if you haven't got a clue how much you'll earn, if anything? In some cases, people take these jobs, do a few deals, and then find that their commission is not forthcoming.

'Goodbye. Get out.'

'But I thought I was doing okay. I've spent a month working for you and I've done three deals. You haven't paid me my commission.'

'That's right. What are you going to do about it? You are not officially employed here. Goodbye.'

It happens.

If you're lucky enough to secure a position with a reputable company who say they're prepared to put you on a contract, the chances of you seeing six months' employment are remote. Many companies will take on staff (say a receptionist or secretary) and tell them it's a trial period but that there will be an official contract available if both parties are happy with each other. This trial period will run on and on, but hardly ever beyond six months. Then, bang – some half-brain excuse and you're down the road and they're ready for the next person. No contract, no rights.

Chris's daughter, Justine, suffered endless times with the 'five-monther'. She liked the jobs and, as far as she was aware, they liked her, but no way were they going to tie themselves in to a full-time contract – goodbye. No work, no money.

Always keep saying this to yourself 'Spain isn't like the UK, so don't pretend that it is'.

I mentioned our beer mat advertising business not working in Spain near the beginning of this book, and just to further illustrate the fact that what works in the UK doesn't follow through over here, I will tell you the following story: One day I got talking to a guy and he told me that he was installing time triggered air fresheners in bar and café toilets. A friend of his in the UK had made a million out of it and he was now bringing the idea to the Costa del Sol. What a great idea I thought; this guy is onto a winner here as I haven't seen anyone else doing it and I know that it is massive business in the UK.

It worked like this – He installed the trigger timing units in the toilets free of charge, one in the gents and one in the ladies. He then charged a monthly rental cost for these triggers and you also had to buy the aerosol fragrances from him. What he didn't take into account, was the fact that there are two distinct differences in bar toilets in the UK to those in Spain.

1.) In the UK, pub toilets tend to be quite large, accommodating a few people at a time.

2.) UK pubs themselves are usually quite large and due to the weather, the outside doors are closed.

In Spain, bars are generally quite small and much smaller than a UK pub. As such, there is usually one small 'one person' toilet for the ladies and one small 'one person' toilet for the gentlemen. As these toilets are just a very small room with just enough room for a toilet bowl and a small sink, the fragrance nearly gasses any visitors in such a small confined space. On top of that, when the toilet door is open, all the fragrance just flies out into the bar area and then straight out onto the street as most bars in Spain are open fronted due to the weather.

Result – After about a month he was asked to take the air fresheners out of virtually every bar where he had installed them, as they were a complete and utter waste of time over here. He must have lost his shirt. You wouldn't think of that one would you?

That was a perfectly good business on the face of it, but what works in the UK doesn't necessarily work over here for reasons you would not normally consider.

Spain is not the UK. If you move over here and do not work, you can sleep in the street or on the beach. There's no going down to the dole office and picking up some money. Forget it. But that's fine; most people have no problem with that whatsoever.

If you come here to retire, you'd be hard pushed to find a better life. If you come here to open a business and make a success of it, the same applies. However, if you come here to open a business and fail, or you just arrive hoping to find a 'proper' job, you will inevitably be very disappointed indeed and struggle badly.

If you even want to get close to securing a proper job in Spain within an office environment, fluent Spanish is a must – and not just verbal. You will have to be able to read, write and type in Spanish. If you have that ability, then you have a chance.

Chapter 13
Beware the cowboys and con men

There are cowboys and con men on the Costa's falling over themselves to rob you. There are electricians who are not really electricians, plumbers who are not really plumbers, refrigeration engineers who are really ex-brickies – you name the profession and there are stacks of Brits claiming to be just that. In many cases, these people are not qualified in anything, but just fell into whatever it is they're doing either by working as a helper to a proper craftsman or by teaching themselves. Don't get me wrong; there are some extremely well-qualified people here, but for every one of them, there are ten cowboys.

One day when we were in our teashop, the washing-up water would not go down the plughole. It's not surprising that this happens every now and again, as bits of lettuce, baked beans and all sorts of stuff gets down there. Also, in Spain, for some reason, they never appear to have a natural fall on waste pipes – they run more or less horizontally. Why is that? It's not logical.

I did the usual: nipped round to the local Arkwright's 100-peseta shop and bought a new plunger. That didn't work, so I then borrowed a drain rod wire from a friend. But that didn't work either. Obviously, if we can't wash up, the business grinds to a halt, so we had to close until the problem was sorted out.

The building in which our business was housed is quite old, and El Presidente of the block liked everyone to use the same Spanish plumber for all work carried out, because he was familiar with the horizontal pipe layout and all the little quirks of the place. Fine. As it happened, this plumber was in the building at the time – there's always something for him to do there and he has nearly a full-time job in that one apartment block.

The plumber appeared about an hour later and set about doing everything I'd already tried, despite the fact that I'd given him a run down of the proceedings to date. Surprise, surprise: he couldn't shift the blockage either. As it was one of the many Spanish saint's days a couple of days later, he said he'd be back with some more equipment to fix it *in about ten days' time*. Pardon? Did I hear that right? Yes, ten days time. That's okay then; we'll just close for ten days until you can get back at your leisure five weeks on Thrumsday. I don't think so.

There are companies over here that call themselves by the same name as reputable companies in the UK even though they have no association with them whatsoever. Looking through a local English newspaper under 'Services', I noticed a company with the same name as a very well known British drain-unblocking company. I was not wise to the way things are at that time, so I wrongly assumed that this must be some kind of franchise, and called the number, which was for a mobile. (I now know that this is a giveaway: if they have no landline, they have no office; and if they have no office, they are a one-man band.)

Sure enough, the guy turned up first thing the very next day and we were looking forward to being back in business by the afternoon. I told him what action had been taken to date and he said he'd have to get something out of his van. He then reappeared with this huge vacuum plunger thing and disconnected the pipes from the sinks and dishwasher, exposing the pipe that went directly into the kitchen wall and down beneath the floor. He pumped this thing over and over again and I could tell by the resistance that this was some blockage. Then – whoosh – blockage gone and water flowing freely down the pipe.

He reconnected the pipes, put more water down in order to prove the point, and I paid him 80 euros for his 15 minutes' work. But it was well worth it, as the blockage was clear now, wasn't it? Err, sort of.

Not 15 minutes later, the janitor and El Presidente came running into our tea shop shouting and waving their arms around like a couple of demented windmills. Calm down, calm down. They were trying to drag me outside, and I thought they were trying to kidnap me, but decided just to go with the flow. Their ranting continued as they led me round the corner, through the underground garage door, down the ramp and into the garage, and finally the cause of their agitation was revealed: El Presidente's mates new Renault Clio was absolutely covered in thick, slimy, gungy shite, and above it was a pipe, hanging down limply through the plasterboard ceiling.

Mr Vacuum-Pumper had cleared the blockage all right. He'd blown the bloody pipe apart, and, rather than all the crap flowing out into the sewage system, it had dropped onto El Presidente's mates new car.

'Err, sorry,' hardly seemed adequate under the circumstances, but what could I say? I don't think El Presidentes mate ever felt the same about that car. (It's a good job it wasn't a soft top.) So in the end it cost us the 80 euros for Mr Vacuum-Pumper, plus the price of a super deluxe car wash, another plumber to re-connect the pipe, and a guy to re-plaster the garage roof. Not one of our better investments!

The Spanish also have their own brand of con men in the form of bogus gas mechanics. They'll walk into your business or come to the door of your home dressed in overalls that are the same colours as the major bottled gas supplier. These guys don't speak English, but they gesticulate in such a way as to make you understand that they wish to view your gas appliances. Then, once they've viewed them, they proceed to make a big deal of cutting the rubber pipe connecting the appliance to the gas bottle, and say, in threatening tones, 'Out of date. Illegal.' They then put on a new length of rubber pipe, get you to sign a form, and take 80 euros off you. You haven't a clue what you've signed, but actually it's a disclaimer saying that you've allowed them to rob you. The 80 euros can vary, depending on how rich you look. Not bad work if you can get it, as that length of pipe costs pennies at the DIY shop. These guys have nothing whatsoever to do with the gas company, and they make an absolute fortune out of this scam day after day. Stripe the Brits, they're easy money.

The other Spanish favourite is the 'fire extinguisher guy', who specialises in visiting bars that have recently changed hands. The new owner hasn't a clue about what's what, so these guys march in and ask to see your fire extinguishers, which you have to have by law. They then shake their heads, lift the extinguishers out of their housings, and take them away, returning a couple of minutes later with different ones: 'You should have changed these before. They are out of date. That's 120 euros please.'

Now, if the bar owner had looked at the labels on the fire extinguishers, he would have seen that they were probably not out of date at all. He would also have seen that this guy wasn't even from the same company as highlighted on the labels of the original extinguishers. Striped again.

Another area that's ripe for the conmen is removals, although we've been lucky. There are many UK-based removal companies that specialise in moving people's furniture from the UK to Spain. We used a company based in Preston, Lancashire, called Movers International, and they were great. They held all our furniture and my brand new Harley Davidson motorbike in their Preston depot and then brought it all over when we made the phone call to let them know that we were ready for it. No problem.

However, if you want to move house once you're living in Spain, there are lots and lots of Brits who are basically 'a man and a van'. Be careful! Ask around and, if at all possible, go with a recommendation. Some are very professional and offer full damage insurance, but more often than not it's literally just a man and a van. Having said that, we found a good one, who I christened 'Hi-top Tom'.

When we moved from our villa in Mijas to an apartment in Riviera del Sol, Tom was recommended to us. He did short-run local removals and had an old Hi-top Transit box van, which looked as if it had taken part in a demolition derby; but he was reliable and did a great job, and we used him three times in total before we bought our own place. What a character. I got talking to him one day during the proceedings over yet another cup of tea and he told me his story. He had owned a very busy and successful fish and chip shop somewhere in the north of England, sold up and moved out to the Costa del Sol to retire. His wife wanted to put a halt to the visual effects of the advancing years, and so persuaded Tom to spend a chunk of their money on some cosmetic surgery, which apparently got a little out of hand. She had a few neck tucks, leg tucks, tummy tucks and then some rather over-the-top breast implants. But Tom was very proud of his new-look wife and told me, 'She looked like a million dollars.' The only problem was that she looked so good that she legged it with a guy 20 years younger than her – a problem that was compounded by the fact that, for whatever reason, their new villa on the coast had been purchased in her name. Result: Tom had to buy a clapped-out van and start doing removals, which was not quite what he had in mind when he moved over here.

He did any fairly small moves himself, but when a full house load needed shifting, he brought along his assistant, who I'll call Tony. Tony was about 25 and didn't look as if he'd had a wash for at least a week, and his clothes were less than fragrant. It sounds unkind to say it, but he was definitely a little short changed in the academic department, and to describe him as strange would be a dramatic understatement. When he first turned up with Hi-top Tom, Tom introduced him to Chris and me, but he just stared at the ceiling and twitched his shoulders. I didn't think much about it, but I did notice as they set to work that whatever Tom asked him to do, he appeared to do completely the opposite.

Every two minutes we could hear Tom saying, 'What the f*** are you doing now? I said do soandso, so why are you doing that?' If they were carrying a large item together, Tom would ask Tony to move left and Tony would move right. If he asked him to lift, Tony would drop. It was a complete fiasco, and we could see that Tom was starting to lose it and, by the time about half a van load of stuff had been taken out of the villa, he disappeared off down the road to cool off, which meant that we were stuck with Tony on our own for a while.

We tried, without success, to get a conversation going with him, and then, all of a sudden, he said nervously, 'I'm in a group you know.'

'Oh, that's good,' I said. 'What kind of music do you play?'

'Our own stuff; mostly heavy rock. It depends on what I've written recently.'

'You write your own songs and music?'

'Oh yes, I write the words and the music, and it's good.'

'It's very difficult to write music isn't it? Where did you learn to do that?'

'I taught myself. I don't write music with those little squiggly thingies. I write it in words.'

'Oh, that's interesting. So how do you convert the sounds into written words?'

'It's easy. It's like "dum der dum, tap, der dop dum". Stuff like that.'

Chris and I looked at each other, struggling not to laugh. But I had to say something.

'Where do you play your music? Do you do gigs at local pubs?'

'In my cellar.'

'Oh, so you practice in your cellar with your friends?'

'No, there's just me in the group at the moment.'

At that point, Tom walked back through the door, and had apparently been listening from the hall.

'What's all this crap about you writing music?' he said. 'You can't even write your own name you toss pot. And what's all this about practising in your cellar? What cellar? You live in a studio apartment on the second floor.'

'Well, I *would* write music if I could, and I *would* practise in my cellar if I had one,' Tony answered, undaunted.

'I rest my case,' said Tom. 'Just pick up the other end of that couch.'

Everyone's interesting in Spain, removal men included!

I sincerely hope that none of you will ever need an undertaker whilst on holiday over here. But beware if you do. We had as regular customers a lovely couple from Liverpool, called Tony and Helen. They came to Fuengirola regularly. They loved the place, and were here so often, and for so long, that they knew just about all the Brits in the west side of town, and were looked upon as ex-pat locals.

Unfortunately, Helen died whilst they were over here during one of their visits. She was a lovely lady, and Tony idolised her. He woke up one night to find that she wasn't beside him, so he went into the hall and found her lying on the hall floor. Very sadly, she'd already passed away. Tony alerted the police and they, in turn, called an undertaker. Not a lot of sympathy from this guy. The first words he spoke to Tony were, 'If you want to take her back to England, it will cost you 6,000 euros.' Poor Helen was still on the floor. Can you believe that?

Things took their course at the undertakers, and then the company in question contacted Tony, informing him that there was a shortfall in the insurance and he'd have to find a further 1,730 euros in cash, immediately; otherwise they would not release Helen's body. Tony coughed up – well he would, wouldn't he? But it transpired that the undertaker had placed Helen in his most expensive coffin, without even asking which coffin Tony would like or whether he had a budget. In circumstances like that, the last thing you're going to argue about is the money it's costing for your wife's coffin, and the undertaker was obviously banking on that – quite literally. No one's really going to turn around and say, 'That coffin is too expensive. You'd better take her out and put her in a cheaper one.'

To make matters worse, a coffin for transport back to the UK has, apparently, got to be metal lined, making it completely useless for cremation. So the coffin was only used for a few days, until the UK undertaker could transfer Helen into another one, and the Spanish undertaker must have known that that would be the case. How cynical can you get?

In order to illustrate just how mercenary this guy was, he then contacted the owner of the apartment Tony and Helen had been renting and said that if anyone else ever died in one of his properties, a phone call to him would secure a kickback of 200 euros a time. What a complete bloodsucker.

On a brighter note, everyone rallied round Tony and made things as good as they could for him to help him cope with the loss of 'his pal', which is what he'd always called Helen. The local Brits chipped in and sent over a beautiful wreath for the funeral in Liverpool.

There's a plant outside the Lounge Bar in Fuengirola, which the owners, Pete and Garry, have tried to kill on numerous occasions, as they didn't like it for some reason. They've tried to pull it up, ripped pieces off it and even poured bleach over it, and everyone thought it was dead. But early on the evening that Helen passed away, she had walked over to the plant, watered it and pulled the dead leaves off, saying that it was a shame to let it die, and that she was sure it would come back to life. Chris and I were there at the time, having a drink with them, so we saw it. I swear to God that within a week of Helen passing away, that plant sprang into life, and it's now a complete picture of health. We all call it 'Helen', and no one's allowed near it.

Chapter 14

Every country has its foibles

They say down here that you should never try to achieve more than one thing per day. I laughed at this when we first arrived; but, believe me, it's true. Us Brits are used to going into somewhere, being served, getting out as quickly as possible and then on to the next task. In Spain, life is not like that. Progress has been, and still is being made, but there is a massive mountain to climb in certain areas of business. The culture over here is different: what's the rush? An orderly queue – what's one of those?

Getting married in Spain

At the time of this episode in our lives Chris and I had been together for more than twenty years but had never got married. We did get engaged around sixteen years ago but never thought it necessary or even important to formally tie the knot. For some reason, I started to think that I would like to pop the question as we were as happy as I thought it was possible for two people to be, and being formally married would finally weld the relationship together. So, on Chris's birthday during December 2007, I told her that we were going out to our favourite Thai restaurant in La Cala de Mijas which is just a couple of kilometres along the coast from our house. Off we went when the evening came, and we went for a drink in the bar opposite the Thai restaurant prior to going for our meal. When we finished our drinks, I suggested to Chris that we went for a quick stroll on the beach just around the corner and she agreed. Once there, staring out to sea and holding hands, I asked her if she would marry me. Her mouth fell open, there was a long pause, and then she said 'yes'.

After a good cry (why did we cry – I haven't a clue), we decided that, under the circumstances, we would go back to the bar and have another drink. This turned out to be a huge mistake as we never actually got to the restaurant. One drink led to another, and then another, and then another, until it became time to pour ourselves into a taxi. I think we had a good evening, but I can't quite remember.

During the next few days we discussed our strategy for the big day and one thing was a cast iron certainty; we wanted to get married in the local white village of Mijas Pueblo. Mijas Town Hall is beautiful inside and a bit Moorish in design, making it a very nice venue and far better than Gibraltar Register Office. Most ex pat Brits who get married over here go to Gibraltar, and I could never understand why as the Register Office is about as basic as you can imagine, and certainly not a very nice setting for a wedding. Anyway, when we announced to our friends that we were getting married and that the venue would be Mijas Pueblo, virtually everyone said 'You won't do it. It's so much hassle that you will finish up getting married in Gibraltar like everyone else. It's so difficult to weave your way through all the red tape that everyone who intends getting married in Mijas sacks it after a while. They go to Gibraltar instead as it's a British ceremony there and simple to arrange'.

Well, that was it. Call me stubborn if you like, but if someone says something like that to me then I'm on a mission and there was no way that I was going to fail and give up on this one. First step: go to Mijas Town Hall and find out exactly what we need in order to book the big day which we wanted to be during July, so that gave us six months. 'That's loads of time isn't it?' Er, no!

Off we go to Mijas Pueblo during January and queued at the Foreign Residents desk to see a very nice lady who talked us through the procedure. She then handed us a printed document highlighting the documents required in order for us to go ahead with the wedding. There are apparently different requirements from different Ayuntamiento's (Councils), so these requirements vary from city to city. There are also different requirements depending on your personal status, such as single, widowed or divorced. As Chris and I were both divorced, the requirements were stated as followed –

Birth Certificate *(Bearing the apostille of the Hague Convention or legalized by the British Consulate, and officially translated into Spanish)*

Inhabitants Certificate *(Issued at the Mijas Town Hall)*

Certificate of previous marriage *(with DIVORCED noted, bearing the apostille of the Hague Convention or legalized by the British Consulate and officially translated. If DIVORCED does not figure, the Divorce Sentence has to* *be added on, also bearing the Apostille of the Hague Convention or legalized and officially translated)*

Certificate of no Legal Impediment *(Issued at the British Consulate)*
N.I.E. (National Insurance Number), Residence or Passport.
Two Witnesses

That seems fairly straightforward then; I think?

First things first: let's just make sure that we have all the relevant certificates in our hi-tech filing system, which was actually a battered cardboard box shoved on a shelf in our garage. God knows where they went to, but I didn't have a birth certificate and Chris didn't have her previous marriage certificate. 'Never mind, we will just have to contact our local Register Offices in the UK and get official duplicates sent over'. That took a couple of weeks and then we had all the British documents required in order to proceed to the British Consulate in Malaga. Off we go to find the British Consulate and I have to say that the people there were great. We explained what we wanted to do, handed over all the relevant documents which would be sent by them to the Foreign and Commonwealth Offices in London, paid 576 euros for the privilege and were asked to return in approximately six weeks as the 'Intention to Marry Notice' had to be displayed on the Consular notice board for a clear 21 days. Sure enough, I called them after about six weeks and they said that all the papers had now returned from London duly stamped, together with the Certificates of No Legal Impediment, and that we could collect them at our leisure.

Next job was the Inhabitants Certificate, which is basically a document confirming that we are actually residents in Mijas Costa. Off to the Town Hall again, and we got bounced around God knows how many people before sitting down in front of a very nice Spanish lady. We gave her our names and address in order for her to generate the necessary document. As she was putting information into her computer, she started to progressively look more and more confused before saying to us –

'You don't own that house'.

'Yes we do, we bought it two and a half years ago'.

'No, I'm afraid you didn't; you are not the actual owners'.

I had an immediate botty flutter! I have lived in Spain for a good few years and know better than most about the horror stories of some Brits who thought they had bought a property but hadn't due to some con or other, so my first reaction was to – er – panic!

'We own that house at that address, we bought it two and a half years ago from a guy called Paco – honest!'

'No, sorry, it can't be your house because the deeds are in someone else's name. Are you sure that you bought it'.

Oh shit, 'Yes, yes, it's our house'. Oh God; should I kill myself now or wait until I get outside?

The lady in question then said, 'This house appears to be owned by a person with a very strange name; he could be Scandinavian or possibly Russian'. She then swivelled her terminal round for us to see the name. I had to look at it for a couple of minutes before I could even begin to pronounce it as it said 'WLLAIM STRAUT RWIGHT'. Then the penny dropped!

'Are you being serious?' I said.

'Yes, of course. That's the name of the person who owns your house'.

The botty twitches had stopped by this time and I said 'My name is Stuart William Wright and it appears that one of your staff either has an affinity to anagrams or my name has been input incorrectly'.

'Oh yes, I see. Tut! This is always happening. Okay' tap tap tap, kerchunk 'Here is your Inhabitants Certificate Mr. Wright. I'm ever so sorry'.

I swear I nearly crawled out of that place on my hands and knees, having nearly poo'd my knickers and almost giving myself a heart attack and a brain hemorrhage.

Anyway, another one down.

With the return of all the stamped and approved UK documents we now had to have them all officially translated into Spanish. There is an 'Approved List' of translators who can be used for this purpose, and of course a company on an 'Approved List' can charge more or less whatever it wants and guess what? It does! What a rip off; 50 euros per page and with the documents being standard, they are almost certainly generated from a template straight off a computer terminal.

By this time I could quite easily understand why virtually everyone sacks it half way through and just goes down the road to Gibraltar.

One by one I knocked them all down, so we went back to the Foreign Residents Department at Mijas Pueblo Town Hall in order to go through everything again, just to make sure that I hadn't overlooked anything.

'That's fine Mr. Wright apart from the fact that we also require copies of the witnesses passports.'

'But that isn't on your list. I didn't know about that'.

'No it isn't is it? We must add that one on'.

Hell; it's a good job we allowed enough time to get through this lot.

A phone call to Chris's daughter Justine, one to my son Oliver, and their passports were scanned and e-mailed across to us within a few days. Off we go again to Mijas Town Hall.

'That's everything in order now Mr. Wright. You can go to the Mijas Court House and present all these papers. They will stamp the relevant papers and these will then have to be sent to Marbella for final approval and your wedding will be confirmed at that time. This will take approximately one month'.

Sure enough, after a month-ish (six weeks actually), everything was confirmed and that was it. A job well done – eventually! It wasn't easy, but if you are determined enough, then it's all very worthwhile.

A Spanish wedding – great!

The banks

The greatest frustration for Brits living in Spain is related to the banks. Banks are a massive topic of conversation, and they are the institutions that people love to hate. It's not that they bombard you with junk mail or are constantly trying to lend you money as in the UK, but most transactions are carried out by a personal visit to the bank. This is very much a cash society and, as such, a visit to the bank is totally necessary for many things.

Now don't get me wrong, most of the bank staff are lovely people; it's just that they've got their priorities completely wrong. There's a definite batting order with bank staff, which is apparent as soon as you walk into many bank branches. There may be two or three cashier desks, but invariably there'll only be one that's occupied – by a junior member of staff. The queue (of sorts) will be twenty deep and will run through the bank to the outside door. Behind the single cashier there'll probably be three or four suited staff trying to look important, laughing, joking and drinking coffee, and not one of them will even think of occupying a vacant cashier desk. In fact, you very much get the impression that to do so would be beneath them.

The amount of time each person spends at the cash desk is also much greater than it would be in the UK, because many people are depositing multiple bills in cash or putting cash from their businesses into the bank, and each transaction seems to take forever. And it doesn't help matters that some of the cashiers chat for several minutes to any customers they know.

That's just the way it is; but if someone opened a proper bank in Spain, they'd clean up.

We had an account with one particular bank, and on a visit to the dreaded cash desk I was informed that they now had Internet banking and would I like to discuss it with one of the behind-the-desk people? Wow, space age for Spain, just what I've been waiting for. About time. Yes, of course I would.

I was shown to the desk of a very nice gentleman, who explained this 'new' technology, of which he was very proud. I received a series of codes and a quick demo' on his screen, and was hugely relieved at the thought that I'd now be able to cut down on my branch visits. A couple of days later, I went into their Internet banking site and viewed our account, with no problems whatsoever.

As it happened, shortly afterwards I wanted to set up a standing order, so I was delighted that I wouldn't have to queue at the branch to do so. But, having played around with the system for a while, I realised that in fact all I could do was look at my account. Although I may be no genius on a computer, I'm no slouch either. But, try as I may, I couldn't do anything other than view our account status. So I telephoned the bank, and eventually spoke to a lady about how to use their Internet banking for transactions etc.

'Oh, no. I'm afraid you can't do that. All you can do at present is view your own account status.'

Oh well, that's really useful. Thanks a bunch. It's archaic!

Banks in Spain also charge high fees. Every time you receive a statement, there are charges for this and charges for that, and some banks actually charge you for putting money in! What's all that about?

Talking about bank statements; you will be very lucky indeed to receive a statement from certain banks over here. For instance: for various reasons we had three bank accounts in Spain at one time, and the last thing we wanted was another one. However, when we bought our apartment the mortgage was arranged through a Spanish bank called the BBVA, so we then finished up with yet another bank account. Also, the branch it was arranged through happened to be in Torremolinos which I thought absolutely nothing about at the time. Oh boy, what a laugh that's been – not! It's only my personal experience, and I guess there must be some Brits who actually like using this bank (I've never met one), but as far as I'm concerned they are worse than useless. The mortgage payment flies out every month without fail and it never appears to be a problem when they want to take money away from you, but getting anything back in return, anything at all, is complete and utter purgatory.

I noticed after a while that I wasn't receiving any statements, so I called into their Fuengirola branch (the nearest branch to my home) and queued as usual to see a man sitting behind a desk. He didn't speak English so I explained in my very best Spanglaise that since I had joined their bank approximately three months ago, I hadn't received even one statement. I was nice and pleasant with him, but he just looked into his computer, tapped a few keys, and wafted me away saying 'Torremolinos, Torremolinos'. I couldn't believe it.

'I just want you to check if the statements are actually being sent out to me or does it require some kind of input into your system in order to trigger the sending out of my statements. Have you got my correct address?'

Waft, waft, 'Torremolinos, Torremolinos. You must go there; here is no good'. He was right about that.

'Surely you don't expect me to drive all the way on to Torremolinos just to check this out do you?'

'Waft, waft, 'Torremolinos, Torremolinos. You must go there. Next please'.

What a complete and utter ignoramus toss pot. Off to Torremolinos then, as I knew from personal experience that it would be a complete and utter waste of time trying to get anything done over the telephone. Off I went the following day to Torremolinos, spent about three hours trying to find a parking spot, and then queued again to see a nice person at my (not so) local branch. What felt like two days, three cans of Coke, and five sandwiches later, I finally got sat in front of a very nice lady who spoke English. I went through the lack of a statement issue with her and she confirmed that I should have had a statement every month since I joined their organization. She went into her computer and we went over my address line by line. 'Yes, that's correct. I can't understand it, but will make sure that you get a monthly statement from now on'.

'Wow; great, thanks!'

That was three years ago, and I still haven't even had one solitary statement.

The only thing for it now is to go down to their Fuengirola branch periodically in order to print out a 'recent movements' slip from their hole in the wall machine. I find myself sneaking in just in case Senor Ignoramus sees me and insists that I can only use the hole in the wall machine at their Torremolinos branch. I have to print the last couple of months account movements out of this machine rather than queue for three days every time I want to know anything about my own money. It's very annoying and very frustrating, but at least the problem's solved now isn't it? No! You may not believe this, but it is completely and utterly true. Approximately half of the occasions I go in to their machine for a statement, I get in return a blank piece of paper because they don't appear to realize that you have to occasionally put some ink into the damn thing – UUUURRRRRRH!

Shrug, shrug, Mañana, mañana. I'll get used to it: I think?

We found the best way was to keep our money in a UK (Channel Islands) account and transfer it over as and when required. The more we could achieve over the telephone and Internet the better.

Land lines

The second greatest frustration for Brits living in Spain is the national telephone company and this prehistoric organization is called Telefonica. They really are living in the dark ages when it comes to customer service. In fact there isn't any customer service. They are by definition a communications company but they haven't got the ability to communicate. They just don't care!

Telefonica are affectionately known to ex pat Brits living in Spain as 'Telefunnyca'.

When we sold The Tea Tree I contacted Telefunnyca asking them to disconnect the land line together with broadband Internet and move it to our apartment. Not too difficult I wouldn't have thought? Some time later an engineer arrived at our apartment, looked around for a suitable place to install the wiring, and then disappeared down the road somewhere. He returned an hour or so later and informed me that there were no spare lines running into our area, and that we couldn't have a line until someone else disconnected.

'Er – aren't you going to run any more lines into this area if there are none available and people are waiting' I asked.

'No' he said.

'Oh, er, okay then, I will have to put my name down on the waiting list I guess. How many people are already on the list in this area?'

'We don't have a waiting list; that's not the way we do it'.

'Okay, what should I do then?' I asked.

'You have to reapply and hope that a line is available at that point in time'.

'No; surely not, are you winding me up?'

'No, that's how it works'.

Oh boy; how daft can you get? There appears to be no logic – again!

'Let me get this right' I said, 'I wait until next month, let's say, apply to you again, you come out and look at your little junction box and tell me that there still isn't a line available and then we go through the whole procedure again and again and again?'

'Yes, that's it'.

'Erm, that doesn't appear to be a particularly cost effective way to run your business if you don't mind me saying so'.

'I know; but it keeps me busy' he said.

What a complete and utter shambles. I had no option but to resort to satellite telephone and Internet. They lost a customer forever and believe me; they have lost many thousands because they don't give a monkeys.

How about this then? Some friends of ours bought a new telephone when they moved into their apartment and plugged it into the landline socket recently reactivated by Telefunnyca. They wanted to use Telefunnyca's answering machine facility but, try as they may, they couldn't put their own message on it. At the time, they had a friend who spoke fluent Spanish so this person played around with it and couldn't get a result either. Rather than continue the frustration, she phoned Telefunnyca and explained the situation asking how her friends could put their own message on the machine as they were British and required an English speaking message.

'You can't do that' said the Telefunnyca man 'Your friends live in Spain so they should be able to speak Spanish'.

'Are you being serious?' said this lady.

'Yes, they live in Spain so they should be able to speak Spanish. As such the message is in Spanish and that's it'.

'But they don't make a habit of phoning themselves. When someone phones them, these people are inevitably phoning from England, and it may surprise you to know that not everyone in England speaks Spanish'.

'Oh yes – er – anyway that's it. You have got a Spanish message. Adios!'

Telefunnyca – what a shambles.

Education

I believe there would be many thousands more Brits moving over to Spain if it wasn't for concerns over their children's education. I agree! In my opinion, there is nothing more important in life than your children's education, and that should be the first priority for anyone considering making the move to Spain. It is a time when the parents should do their homework instead of the children.

Education in Spain is no different to education in the UK insofar as some schools are better than others. The one massive difference of course is the fact that Spanish schools obviously conduct their business and classes in the native Spanish language. Don't worry; you won't be alone, as there are many thousands of families living here on the Costa´s from the UK, Holland, Germany, Denmark and just about any other northern European nation you care to name. On top of that, there is a large Moroccan population, together with people from the ex Spanish south American colony countries.

Most children in Spain attend nursery school from the ages of 3 to 5 years, but there are also many nurseries who take very young children from the age of 1 year. If you look carefully, you will also find the odd nursery which is prepared to take fairly young babies. They then move to their primary school from the age of 6 and stay there until they are 12 years old. Some children (often Brits because they haven't sufficiently mastered the Spanish language) repeat a year in primary school because they haven't reached the standard required. Classes are mixed ability and national exams do not exist in the same way as they do in England. Also, state schools rarely have a uniform code.

Nurseries - I guess the best time to relocate to Spain with children is when they are very young. Very young children won't even realize that they have moved away from the UK. As long as mummy and daddy are with them everything's fine – what's changed? There are many UK run nurseries, but there are also lots of excellent Spanish run nurseries 'Guarderia Infantil'. All the British people I know who have very young children have chosen the Spanish nurseries as their children are then surrounded by the Spanish language from a very early age, and therefore pick it up very quickly 'accent and all'. Young tots won't have a total command of the English language anyway, so if they are suddenly surrounded by children speaking Spanish, then in no time at all they start coming out with basic Spanish words naturally such as agua 'water', hola 'hello' etc. etc. It doesn't take long before they are part of the little Latin gang.

There is a considerable choice of British run nurseries on the Costa´s but these do tend to be considerably more expensive than the Spanish ones. Don't forget also, that you as grown ups, will probably be able to get by with a basic command of the Spanish language but once your child gets into the proper school, he or she will have a massive advantage if they have a basic grounding in the language to start with. Being surrounded by Spaniards from an early age will help tremendously once they start proper school. Think it through! Think one step ahead. What will be your next step after the nursery days are over? Will you be sending your child to a private English speaking school or a Spanish state school? If it is the latter, then a Spanish nursery will be a good grounding.

Beware of the language barrier though. Never, ever underestimate the problems and frustrations you will experience if you don't speak Spanish, and the chances are that when you first arrive in Spain you won't be able to. For example: A couple who are friends of ours put their daughter Libby into a Spanish nursery and were delighted with it as she settled in very quickly. At the time, they were trying to potty train Libby, and the lady tried desperately to explain this to the Spanish nursery staff. Every morning they would take the little girl to nursery wearing pull up pants and every evening she would be collected wearing a disposable nappy. Whenever the nursery staff saw Libby's mum, they would be extremely friendly towards her even though she couldn't understand one single word they said, and she also got the impression that they were very reluctant to take her money off her when payment time came. Time after time she tried to explain that she didn't want the disposable nappies on Libby as she was attempting to potty train her, but every night she collected her, a new fresh nappy would be on again. One day they decided that Libby's dad would drop her off as he spoke a little Spanish and he would attempt to resolve the situation. It transpired that the staff had interpreted Libby's mums 'Spanglaise' and gesticulations as meaning that unfortunately she couldn't afford nappies, hence the pull up pants. They felt sorry for her and put Libby in a new clean nappy every day prior to collection. 'Poor souls, they can't afford nappies for their child'.

Needless to say, these people were extremely embarrassed as for the last two months the nursery staff had assumed they were well on the breadline and tried to help them out by force-feeding them disposable nappies.

It's not just at the nursery school where the language issue kicks in either. Another couple we know have a little boy and after only a few weeks at the local Spanish primary school, he came home with an envelope containing a letter from the school which was, of course, in Spanish. They read it and could just about make out that it was referring to a Fiesta on the following Monday. 'Oh, there's a party at Josh's school next Monday'. It is quite normal when there is a Fiesta in Spain to dress the children up, so they went to the trouble of going out and buying him a Batman outfit (not very Spanish but there you go). There he was, all excited and chomping at the bit over the weekend about the school Fiesta on the Monday. Unfortunately, what the parents hadn't realized is that 'Fiesta' is a double meaning word in Spanish. It can mean 'party' but it can also mean 'holiday'.

Yes, that's right, when they arrived at the school gates the following Monday with little Josh dressed up like the caped crusader, the school gates were locked and there wasn't another child in sight – oops!

Then there's the food. We adults are quite used to the names of foreign dishes, but not so young children. If your child attends a Spanish state school, when you ask him or her what they have had for lunch, there isn't a chance in hell that they are going to reply 'Shepherds pie and mash' or 'Egg, chips and beans'. We were talking to another couple we know some time ago and they told us the story of their experience with the 'foreign food kid'. The lady collected her boy from primary school one day and enquired where his socks were, as he was wearing socks when she dropped him off in the morning.

'They're in my school bag with a surprise', said the boy.

'What do mean "with a surprise?"'

'Well' said the boy, 'for lunch we had tortle'.

'Tortle - do you mean turtle?'

'Er, well it might have been turtle, but it didn't look or taste like a turtle'.

'You have never eaten turtle before, so how would you know'.

'Well it didn't have crunchy shell bits in it, but I didn't like it anyway'.

'Did you eat it?'

'Yuk no, but I had to pretend that I ate it, and I thought you would like it'.

'Oh, so did you bring a little bit of it home for me to try?'

'I brought quite a lot of it home and that's why I haven't got any socks on'.

'What's "tortle" got to do with you not having any socks on?'

'Well, I couldn't think of any way to bring it home for you, so I took my socks off and put it in one of those. Look'.

His mother took a filled soggy sock out of his school bag and looked inside. It was the remnants of a tortilla'.

'Oh, thanks, that's very nice, but I think I'll eat it later if you don't mind'.

Moving on. Once your children reach school age, or if they are already at school age when you make the move, you will basically have two choices –

The state school - Depending on their age, children are like sponges and take in language changes much easier than adults do. It's very difficult for parents to just throw their child or children into a foreign school, but surprising how quickly they adapt to a totally different language and environment. I have seen parents crying their eyes out because they have looked through the school gates at play time during their child's first week or so, and seen them standing on their own in a corner of the playground whilst all the other children play happily around them. It doesn't take long though before they are jabbering away at home in fluent Spanish and bringing round their little Spanish friends. It's a joy to watch. It's difficult at first but they adapt, and I think it's great that British people have the nerve to send their children to Spanish state schools. Approximately 80% of British expats send their children to state schools in Spain.

It can't be easy, but once the initial heartache is over, the British children become part of their own little Spanish society and are also a godsend when Mum and Dad need an interpreter.

'Oh dad, why do I always have to explain everything in Spanish?'

'Er, its good practice for you son'. Liar!

The private school - I obviously cannot comment on every part of Spain but certainly along the Costa del Sol in southern Spain, there are a number of excellent British private schools. There are also private German schools, French schools, Norwegian schools; you name it. British schools teach the British curriculum preparing pupils for GCSE's, A levels and University entrance. Demand is high for places though, so apply as far in advance as possible. Believe it or not, some of the British schools have such a good reputation that many 'well to do' Spanish families actually send their children to them as they are also anxious for their children to be fluent in English, which is the first language at most of these British schools. This can be looked upon as a disadvantage to British people moving over here depending on your outlook. If you live in Spain and your children are probably going to spend the rest of their lives in Spain, then wouldn't they be better off going to a school where Spanish is the first language? It's down to personal choice, but something that requires thinking through very carefully.

Healthcare

If you intend working in Spain or opening a business in Spain, then one of the first things you need to do is go down to the local town hall (in some areas it's the police station) and apply for an NIE (National Insurance) number. This entitles you to work, and also doubles up as a residents identity card. Prior to doing this, lie down in a dark room for a few days, prepare a thermos flask of tea or coffee, and also a bucket load of sandwiches as you will probably be in there forever. Depending on your chosen destination, there will probably be a queue for three hundred metres full of Brits, Germans, Moroccans, Peruvians, Ecuadorians, and god knows who else. Some of these places issue you with a ticket and depending on where you are in the batting order, you can go for a walk for an hour or seven until your number is somewhere near the front. If you have a few euros to spare, you can blag your way in as inevitably outside these ticket issuing offices there will be entrepreneurial people selling low number tickets. What they do is arrive first thing in the morning and secure a ticket. They then keep rejoining the queue in order to secure another ticket and another and another. Meanwhile one of their mates will be selling the first tickets to someone at the back of the queue. What a great idea – I wish I had thought of that!

Anyway, once you have completed the relevant paperwork you will be eligible to secure work. Once you secure a job or open your own business then you will pay National Insurance and that will automatically entitle you to healthcare. BE CAREFUL if you are offered a job which is 'cash in hand' and many of them are over here. If you are paid 'cash in hand' then you will not be in the system!

In addition to the public health system, there are also numerous non-public 'pay as you go' hospitals which are also in the private medical network, and these have very high medical standards indeed.

The situation in Spain is similar to the UK insofar as most Spaniards are covered for health treatment by the public healthcare system, but many have also chosen to go private in order to avoid waiting lists and having the ability to choose a hospital.

Doctors - Before you choose a Doctors practice to register with, speak to a few people and go with a recommendation wherever possible. Don't get me wrong, the doctors over here are, generally speaking, excellent but many are unable (or unwilling) to speak English and if you have only just arrived in Spain then your conversation can be one hell of a laugh. You can always point to the problem but lets just say the problem exists on your naughty bits then what are you going to do about that?

Dentists - All dental practices in Spain are private. You pay for absolutely everything but it is, generally speaking, cheaper than private dental treatment in the UK. If you choose to move into the countryside then inevitably you will have to go with a Spanish dentist. If, however, you take the more popular route of choosing one of the Costa´s, then you will have a fantastic choice of very good dentists. There are British dentists, Dutch dentists, Scandinavian dentists; you name it. Don't be worried about dental care in Spain because it is at least as good as you will receive in the UK.

Many people have very serious hang-ups about dentists and I know you probably won't believe me, but the dentists over here really are very good. I remember when we first moved over here, I had visions of a dental surgery resembling a butchers shop. A large wooden chair with straps over each arm and the front legs, a big mallet for smacking you over the head with, and a rusty Black and Decker drill on the floor. It's not like that – honest!

State run hospitals - The public healthcare system in Spain is at least as good (and often better) than you will be used to in the UK. Standards and availability vary dramatically across the country but the more popular Costa´s are covered to a high standard. This is something you need to consider if you are moving inland chasing a 'back to basics' lifestyle, as your options will be very limited. Also, you will be very lucky indeed to find anyone who speaks English (or wants to). On the Costa´s however, many of the state run hospitals are excellent and there will inevitably be some English speaking staff or at least an interpreter. The main difference between UK state healthcare and Spanish state healthcare is the level of nursing care. Spanish nurses do not carry out many of the duties taken for granted by UK nurses such as personal care and feeding. These tasks are usually carried out by the patient's family as many hospitals allow one family member or friend to be with the patient 24 hours a day with standard visiting hours applying to other visitors.

Private hospitals - Most ex pats living in Spain consider British private schemes offer better healthcare cover than Spanish policies. There are numerous UK companies offering healthcare cover in Spain and the best way to make your choice is to study their literature and question them if you are unsure on the levels of cover. BUPA for instance, own Spain's biggest private health insurer 'Sanitas'. Once you have made your decision then inevitably you will have a good choice of hospitals and these are excellent.

It's your choice, public or private. Just to give you an idea of how highly the state hospitals on the Costa del Sol are regarded, Chris and I do not consider paying to go private is worthwhile. Also, our Gestoria (Accountant), who isn't short of a bob or two, doesn't consider paying for his family to go private either!

Middle diddle - There are in certain areas of Spain organizations which offer a half way house between public and private healthcare. I believe this is the way to go over here. On the Costa del Sol we have two major players in the form of Angeles Nocturnos (Night Angels) and Helicopteros. We are with Night Angels and at the time of writing they charge an initial (one off) joining/membership fee of 80 euros per person. The cost thereafter is 167.40 euros per year (about 3 euros a week each). Night Angels offer a number of services and virtually all of their staff speak English. You can call them out to your home in emergency 24 hours a day 365 days a year. You can also visit their surgery any time you like without having to make an appointment and be seen by an English speaking doctor (male or female). It really is money well spent and tremendous peace of mind knowing that they are at the other end of a telephone any time you want them. When Chris and I joined, she mentioned to the lady filling out our forms that she was having pains in one of her fingers. That was it, we had hardly handed over our joining fee when Chris was whizzed into a side room and given three x-rays. Shortly afterwards a lady doctor talked her through the x-rays, gave her a prescription and we were out again within about half an hour.

They also provide dental treatment which is excellent. Six monthly check ups are free with significant discounts given on treatment depending on what it is.

Middle diddle – It's not a compromise; its excellent value for money!

The siesta

The opening hours of Spanish businesses can be very confusing. The *siesta* is an integral part of Spanish life, and many shops and businesses still close for two or three hours during the afternoons. Inevitably, if something goes wrong and you require immediate assistance, or you run out of something and need an instant replacement, it's *siesta* time.

Say it's 2.30 p.m. and you need to speak to someone regarding business or money. You have no chance, no chance at all. You might be lucky and catch them at 4 o'clock, but it's more likely to be 5 o'clock. In years gone by, you can understand working people wanting to get out of the summer heat for a couple of hours' sleep and re-emerge at 5 o'clock to work in a more tolerable temperature. But these days most offices, shops and businesses have air conditioning, and many people commute considerable distances to work. But *siesta* is tradition; it's the Spanish way of life.

We live in their country and respect that, but I just cannot get my head round, say, a shop assistant finishing at 2 o'clock every afternoon, getting into his or her car, driving home, getting into bed for a sleep and then getting back to work for 5 o'clock. How much sleep would they get anyway? What's the point?

Rain stops play – I mean work

One element that grinds the wheels of industry to a halt is the rain. If it's raining and you need to try to get someone to fix something – forget it.

We once had a problem with the hot water in a villa we rented. It was during a particularly wet spell in the winter, and we spoke to the agent, who promised to get a guy out to fix it. This particular agent used the same Spanish guy for just about any job requiring attention in any of his properties. Having no hot water during a cold spell is not pleasant, and we waited in all the following day, but the guy never arrived – what a surprise! This went on for four days, during which time we were boiling water in kettles, pans and anything else we could lay our hands on. When he did eventually arrive, I asked where the hell he'd been. He looked surprised and, as though he was explaining something to a rather backward child, said, 'It's been raining, so I couldn't work.' Eh?

When it rains, roads turn into rivers and rivers turn into waterfalls. Everything stops. Storm drains – what are those?

The receipt game

An example of the silly and irritating things you can fall for is the 'lack of receipt' game, which is a favourite game played by many Spaniards. I fell for this one, but got away with it, thankfully.

When we first opened our business, the previous owners introduced us to an English guy who was an insurance broker. They'd got their business insurance through him and he was recommended. So this guy gave us a price and, as one does, we obtained two or three alternative quotations from insurance companies we'd seen advertised in the local press. His price was there or thereabouts, so we went with him, and arranged to meet him at the offices of a fairly large insurance company in Fuengirola in order to fill out the necessary forms. This we did, paid the cash, and walked out with a certificate.

Not uncommon for over here, but this insurance broker disappeared, and so when the insurance was due again the following year, I telephoned the insurance company to secure a price for the renewal. Fortunately, there was a Scandinavian woman working in the office who spoke English, so she gave me the details of the premium and we agreed I'd call in later that week.

When I got to the office, I searched out the Scandinavian lady and she told me to go to the Spanish guy sitting opposite her, give my name and he would sort me out – fine. I gave my name, he found the insurance certificate, I handed over the money and away I went.

A few days later, I received a phone call from the same insurance company asking me when I was going to pay the premium.

'Pardon? I have paid the premium. I paid it when I collected the certificate.'

But they were absolutely adamant that, 'according to our records', the premium had not been paid.

That evening, I went round to the offices again and spoke to the guy who I took to be in charge. He spoke a little English.

'No sir, the premium has not been paid. Do you have a receipt?'

Hang on a minute! 'I have the insurance certificate. It's here, look. How come I have got this if I haven't paid the premium? You wouldn't have given me this without having first received the money.'

'No, sorry, we issue renewal certificates automatically, sometimes through the post, and if the premium is not paid shortly afterwards, we assume the customer does not require renewal and cancel the policy.'

'But you must reconcile monies at the end of each day. Surely your takings must have been up that day. You must keep records.'

He shrugged his shoulders, which roughly translated seemed to mean that he couldn't give a toss. I was fuming, and I went over to the guy who I'd given the cash to, but he just shook his head and waved me away.

That was it; I'd lost it. I hate being robbed. We were talking about a few hundred euros here, not just the price of a pint.

Next, I marched over to the Scandinavian lady. I was shouting by now, having gone into full lunatic mode.

'It was only a few days ago. You must remember. I came in to pay a premium and you asked me to go and see that guy there. Yes, him; the one who's keeping his head down.'

'Yes, I do remember you, and yes, I did see you pay him.'

Thank Christ for that. The lady spoke to the manager in Spanish and his expression suddenly changed from calm to very annoyed. He went over to the cash guy and gave him a right ear bashing, and then turned to me and said in broken English, 'Sorry, there has been a mistake. All is okay and we hope to see you again next year.'

Fat f***ing chance of that!

The cash guy had trousered my money – and how many other times had he done it?

The moral of the story is: whatever you buy or pay for, absolutely whenever you hand over money, get a receipt. Insist, stand there until you get one, but get a receipt.

While we're on the subject of insurance, when our insurance did expire, I contacted another insurance company and made an appointment to go in and see them, with a view to moving our business over to them. I sat down at the desk of a very nice Spanish gentleman and explained what I wanted, as well as the problems I'd experienced with the previous company.

'Okay,' he said, speaking in heavily accented English. 'Can we just go through a few things in order for me to give you a quotation?'

Of course. No problem.

'How many square metres are your premises?'

'Approximate value of fixtures?'

'Do you have gas or are the premises all electric?'

'How many hands?'

Pardon?

'How many hands?'

Sorry?

'How many hands have you got?'

For some reason, I glanced down to check. 'Er, two.'

'Only two? Okay. What year and manufacturer are they?'

'What year are they? Well, they're my own hands, so they're the same age as me.'

I was getting annoyed, although it began to seem likely that there'd been some misunderstanding between us. But the insurance broker was becoming very obviously impatient.

'I need to know how many hands you have and what age they are,' he said slowly and irritably.

'Two hands,' I shouted. 'Look!' and I waved them in front of his face. 'How many hands did you expect me to have?'

'No, no, no,' he said, the light obviously dawning. 'Not hands – HAMS.'

If you've ever been to Spain, or any other Mediterranean country for that matter, you'll probably have seen the cured hams hanging from the ceiling in cafés and bars. Some of them, depending on the vintage, are worth an absolute fortune and have to be included in the insurance. But how the hell was I supposed to know?

Change slamming

Why do Spaniards do that? I genuinely believe that it isn't malicious, but it infuriates me. In the UK, if you pay a shop assistant for something, 99 times out of 100 he or she will take your money and hand you back your change. But for some reason – which I will never understand – it doesn't work like that in Spain. You hand over your money, the shop assistant puts it into the till, takes out your change, and then SLAMs it down on the counter in front of you, even if you're standing there with your hand out. Is it because they're reluctant to risk touching your hand and potentially catching some horrible contagious disease? I used to take exception to change slamming, assuming it was something that was only done to tourists because they didn't like us, but if you stand back and watch for a few minutes, you'll see that it's done to everyone. So it can't be malicious, can it?

Pedestrian bridges

When is a pedestrian bridge not a pedestrian bridge? Answer: when it has scooters and motorcycles going over it.

How on earth do they get away with that? There you are, minding your own business, walking over a footbridge, when all of a sudden a scooter or ten will come towards you. Quite rightly, footbridges that are built these days have ramps rather than steps so that they're wheelchair friendly. But what happens? People ride bikes, scooters and motorcycles across them, and there's nothing you can do about it – except jump out of the way as they hare towards you.

In the UK, I think I'm correct in saying that these scooter-footbridge-type people would be lucky to get halfway across before they were either booked by a bobby or smacked in the mouth by some urban vigilante. But, in Spain, people don't seem to mind; they just appear to accept it as part of everyday life and let them get on with it.

The trip switch

Ask anybody who has spent any reasonable amount of time in Spain and they will tell you all about the trip switch. It drives people to suicide. What's wrong with Spanish electricians? With very few exceptions, there can't be enough electrical power going into Spanish properties. Or is it just that the Brits use more appliances than the Spanish? If so, why? I still can't understand it.

Every property we've lived in with the exception of one (which must have been near a power station) has had this bloody infuriating problem. You put the kettle on, fine. You then put a slice of bread in the toaster, probably fine. Your wife then turns the iron or her hair dryer on – and CLICK, there it goes, the trip switch in the electricity junction box. It appears that two electrical appliances are the maximum you're allowed to use at any one time. CLICK, CLICK, BLOODY CLICK all the time.

Most properties have worn-out marble tiles directly in front of the junction box, because that's where people spend most of their time. If you have a tumble drier or washing machine turned on, you may as well just go and sit on a stool at the junction box for the full duration. Most of these boxes have a door covering the actual trip switches, and I can almost guarantee that if you look at any property that isn't brand new, the junction box door will be either bent or completely broken.

That's because most men spend half their lives whacking the bastard thing out of sheer frustration.

Solar panels

Where are they? What's wrong with this place? The sun is the biggest asset they have. It's up there in the sky most of the day, most of the time. Even when the sun isn't actually there, it's never far away, and yet you could spend all day driving around the Costa del Sol and would be lucky to see two solar panels. In the UK, when the fog clears for a moment, you can see solar panels on council houses in Leeds. It isn't logical.

I've asked Spanish people on numerous occasions why they don't have solar heating, and they've just shrugged and said, 'I don't know.'

I've already mentioned the fact that most properties are damp in the winter, and solar panels would sort this out. Once you've paid for installation, your electricity's provided for free by the old currant bun. It may be that companies have tried to sell solar heating in Spain but haven't made a very good job of it. Did they price it wrongly? I don't know. But I cannot believe that there isn't a British entrepreneur out there who could rustle up a few good salesmen and start whacking them in. A great opportunity awaits someone.

El Banditos

Crime does not appear to be a massive problem on the Costa's, or at least not in my personal experience. It is there though, and it comes in various guises.

The opportunists. These are the people who 'sus out' who's sitting on the terrace of a bar or café in the summer. They work in twos, and if there's someone sitting there with a juicy-looking bag or a phone, they will come in and sit at the next table. They usually just order a coffee or a soft drink and do one of two things: either sit there until the people on the next table are preoccupied and then leg it with the bag or phone, or operate 'the blag'. The favourite blag involves getting out a large paper map and then one of them asking the people at the next table if they know where 'so and so' is. While one is doing this, and unfolding the map in front of these poor people's faces, the other one is dipping the bag or pocketing the phone.

The gypsy flower-selling dippers. Now these people are cynical. They prey on the elderly and don't give a damn that in most cases they ruin people's holidays and, at worst, could even give some poor victim a heart attack. They are women, and usually operate in twos or threes. One of the women will walk up to an unsuspecting elderly person and push a bunch of flowers or herbs in front of his or her face. While the flowers or herbs are halfway up the person's nose, the flower seller's other hand will be dipping the bag. They are good, very good. I lost count of the number of times old ladies would come into our teashop and tell us they'd been robbed by one of these people – purse, passport, everything.

The Moroccan-looking guys. If you ask anyone on the Costa´s who they believe commit the majority of crimes, most will say 'the Moroccan-looking guys'. They are the opportunists, the people who smash car windows to steal something on the seat, the burglars and the late-night muggers. I've only had one encounter with these guys and, looking back, I guess I could have finished up in hospital. But I hate people who rob me.

One morning, after putting out the tables and chairs on our terrace, I nipped round the corner to the local bakery, which I did every morning. As I returned and came round the corner, these two Moroccan-looking guys were crossing our terrace laughing, and had obviously just come out of our teashop.

I went in and asked Chris, 'What did those two want?'

She'd been in the kitchen, so she hadn't seen anyone, but, looking around, she suddenly said, 'Where are our cigarettes? They were on the bar.'

Never mind the cigarettes, where's my lighter? My son, Oliver, had bought me a Ted Baker Zippo lighter for my birthday, and it meant a lot to me. These two tossers had just walked in, seen there was nobody around, nicked the cigarettes and lighter, and then just walked out again, laughing.

Because of the lighter, it was personal, and I had a rush of steam to the head and legged it after these two guys. I caught up with them fairly quickly, which wasn't easy in a pair of flip-flops, and I stuck my hand out and asked for the cigarettes and lighter. The old 'two onto one' move slipped into gear, as the one on the left took a step to the side so that one of them was directly in front of me and the other one was to my left. Here we go; I've been here before, albeit many years ago.

As it happened, he hadn't pushed the Lambert and Butler packet down into his pocket, and the packet top was visible. I slowly slipped off my flip-flops, one at a time, took a step backwards, and pointed to the packet in his pocket, saying as I did so, 'Give them back.'

Now, most of these guys carry knives, so they must have thought I was either a lunatic or a karate expert (or both). The guy in front of me took the cigarettes out of his pocket and handed them to me. If they were going to make a move, it would come now; but, much to my surprise, it didn't. At my insistence, he also gave me the lighter, and, muttering 'Thieving bastards,' I turned and walked away, trying to look hard, but breathing ferociously.

It was a stupid thing to do, and I could have come to grief, but why should you just let someone walk into your premises, take your property, and then let them go?

A classic. A Dutch friend of ours called Jacob, who lived near our teashop, kept having a read of parts of this book whilst I was writing it, and he'd give me his opinion. He has lived in Spain for many years, speaks perfect Spanish, reads the Spanish newspapers and gets Spanish books from the library.

One day, after reading part of it, he said, 'There's a book by a Spaniard about Spanish scams, thefts and swindles. It includes one section on a man who managed to sell a whole Spanish village that didn't belong to him to a property developer. You would like it, and you may find it useful for your own book. I will go to the library, get it out, and translate the parts of interest into English.'

'Well, thanks Jacob; that would be great.'

This guy came back to me a couple of days later, grinning from ear to ear. 'I went to the library yesterday and the book is on their computer as being in stock, but it isn't there – someone has nicked it.' Someone had stolen a book about stealing!

The language

One thing we Brits are incredibly guilty of is not bothering to learn the language. People can say what they want, but in the cold light of day it comes down to one thing, PURE LAZINESS! It's arrogant. You come to live in a foreign country, can't be bothered to learn the language, and then are actually disappointed if you try to communicate with locals and they don't speak English. If you went to live inland at a small village, you'd have no choice but to learn the language. If you didn't speak Spanish, not only would you not get anything done, but you wouldn't stand a chance of being accepted.

But there are so many Brits on the Costa´s that in reality you don't have to be able to speak Spanish: whatever you want, there is a Brit who supplies it. There are lots of retail businesses that are owned by Brits – everything from butchers to furniture shops to double-glazing sellers. Also, many Spanish people are all too aware of how important British money is to their lives and jobs. Some may not admit it, but the Spanish know they need the Brits just as much as the Brits need the Spanish. So, many of the major Spanish outlets go out of their way to recruit sales staff who can speak English. If you go into one of the huge furniture retailers or DIY outlets, you will almost always find at least one member of staff who speaks perfect English, and signs in the shop will sometimes be in both languages.

I believe that the reason why there is so little resentment towards us invaders is that the Spanish know that we bring our own money into their country and claim very little back, if anything. Okay, we use their schools and hospitals, but most Brits pay National Insurance, are legally within the system, and pay their way.

All of this combined means that the Brits don't have to speak Spanish. It shouldn't be the case, but that's the way it is. We know lots of people who started out with good intentions and began having Spanish lessons. But, within a few weeks at most, they jacked it in, for whatever reason. I take my hat off to anyone who has a go at the language.

If you are one of the majority of Brits who don't have Spanish lessons, you invariably pick the language up as you go along – an odd word here, another one there, words from advertising posters etc. The best thing to do is start off slowly – go into a shop and instead of pointing or asking for something in English, have a go. Don't be afraid to get it wrong; the Spanish are usually very pleased that you're trying. Be careful though: as with any language, there are some words that are similar to others but have completely different meanings – and some are embarrassing if you get them wrong.

For instance, there's *huevos* (pronounced webbos) meaning eggs. On the other hand, *jueves* (pronounced webbes) means 'Thursday. If you're not careful, you can ask for 'half a dozen Thursdays', or tell someone, 'I'll meet you at seven o'clock on eggs.'

Then there's the Spanish word for a box or crate, which is *caja* (pronounced caca). On the other hand, the word *kaka* means the same as it does in certain parts of the UK. Here again, you could innocently get this completely wrong and tell a supplier, for example, that you want your vegetables in shit.

Chris's daughter, Justine, can speak fluent Spanish, but a couple of years ago a simple visit to the meat counter in a supermarket proved to be so embarrassing for her that she has never been back to the shop. Chicken in Spanish is *pollo* (pronounced poyo), whereas *poya* means 'dick' or 'knob' – call it what you want, but you get the message. 'Could I have some dick please' is perhaps not the best introduction to trying out your language skills in front of seven or eight elderly Spanish ladies.

Also, be careful if you say 'American' to a Spaniard. 'American', if said quickly, can sound like *maricón*, which is fine if you actually are gay, although, even so, your sexuality may not be something you wanted to discuss with the cashier in the bank or the young, attractive Spanish woman at the bus stop.

If in doubt, gesticulate – although that can be confusing too.

I don't know if it's a good thing or a bad thing, but I have never been afraid of making a fool of myself if I want something. If you don't speak the language and the person you're trying to communicate with doesn't speak English, then what can you do other than gesticulate? When we first arrived in Spain, I often did this, and yes, I did make a fool of myself. These are a couple of examples I still remember.

I went into a fishmonger's one day, wanting to buy two swordfish steaks. I didn't have half a clue what 'swordfish' was in Spanish, so I said *pescado*, which is the Spanish word for fish. I then proceeded to raise my right arm in front of my nose in a gesture that I thought indicated a swordfish, but which in fact was probably more reminiscent of a lop-sided Nazi salute. Understandably, the woman looked at me as though I'd just escaped from a secure unit somewhere and, while slowly edging away towards the back of the shop, called two guys in from the storeroom. Off I go again, 'swimming' around the shop while doing my swordfish impersonation and getting quite carried away with my newly discovered miming skills. By this time, a couple of locals had come in, and they too looked at me nervously, while staying close to the only visible exit.

Pause. 'Ah, elephant!' one of the guys said triumphantly. What? I'd never thought of that, but surely the fact that I was in a fishmonger's made it unlikely I'd be asking for elephant. But I could see that the head nodding that was now taking place was an attempt to convey to me the fact that they didn't sell elephant. So I shrugged my shoulders, said 'Gracias' and walked out, leaving them to their discussion, which, had I heard it, I'm fairly sure would have enabled me to learn the Spanish word for 'tosser'.

A similar thing happened just days after we arrived down here, when I didn't speak even one word of Spanish. We were in a mini-market in a small village, so the English was non-existent. I wanted some eggs, but as far as the lady behind the counter was concerned, I could have been asking for an aircraft carrier. There I go, bent legs, arms folded to resemble wings and hands on hips, doing what I considered to be a rather good chicken impression, stopping every so often to drop my arse as if laying an egg. 'Ah, huevos.' It worked that time!

As with any other language, there are some aspects of Spanish that seem illogical to a native English speaker, such as the following, to take only a few examples.

The letter J isn't a J at all. It's pronounced as something between an H and a K – a sort of back of the throat Kkkhhhhh.

The letter V exists as a written letter but not as a sound: it's pronounced as a B.

Confused? You will be.

The word 'the' in the English language is just 'the' – that's it, pure and simple. However, in Spanish, it can take a number of forms, including 'el', 'la', 'los' and 'las'.

The word 'the' is often preceded by the word 'of', i.e. 'of the'. In Spanish, 'of the' can be 'de la', 'del', 'de los' or 'de las'.

What about a double L? In English, LL is a strongly pronounced L. However, in Spanish, LL is pronounced Y.

Why? I don't know. That's just the way it is – and it's one of the reasons why so many Brits give up with their Spanish lessons. But think about it. There are a hell of a lot more Spaniards who speak English than there are Brits who speak Spanish, and English isn't any easier for them than Spanish is for us (I think!). It's just that they persevere, which can't be easy when you consider the many quirks of English, such as the following.

'I before E except after C.' So it's receive, conceive and deceive but believe, relieve and sieve (which is pronounced 'siv') – and I doubt very much that that seems logical to a Spaniard learning English.

And what about 'There', 'Their' and 'They're' – which all sound exactly the same but mean completely different things
Or take 'ph', which in reality is a 'f'…

There are lots and lots of examples, not to mention all the words that have two meanings, like 'present'. So all languages have their oddities, and perseverance is the only way to learn them. But don't take any notice of me, because I still can't speak Spanish fluently!

British bars

There are many excellent British bars along the Costa´s. There are sports bars, Irish theme pubs, illegal betting bars, jazz bars, blues and soul bars, the lot. I'm sorry to say, however, that *some* of the British-owned bars are complete dustbins, owned and run by people who either can't be bothered or genuinely haven't got a clue. They are a disgrace, and make a massive contribution to giving the Brits a bad name.

At least in the UK the major pub chains operate a training programme for new staff and, presumably, if they're completely useless, they're out. But you can go into literally hundreds of bars over here and the tables are permanently sticky, the spirit bottles on the shelves are covered in dust, the mirrors are so dirty that you can't see anything reflected in them, and you wouldn't let your dog use the toilets. Why? It shouldn't be so. Most of the time these bar owners have absolutely nothing to do because hardly anyone goes in. So why don't they spend their time cleaning? They've thrown in the towel and just lean on the bar reading a newspaper with a self-filling pint in front of them. Sometimes the bar owners are so pissed, so often, that they'll pay some unfortunate person a pittance to look after their bar for a few hours a day while they sleep it off.

We got to know a guy who's deaf and whose speech is bad due to this, but he can lip read perfectly. He was desperate for a job, as he'd come over with a limited amount of money and had got to the point of urgently having to generate some cash. He started frequenting a particular bar, and the locals thought he was great. Now, a deaf barman is not a common sight anywhere, but the owners of this bar offered him a job for just a couple of hours a day so that they could have a *siesta*. He was elated. What they were paying him was really taking the mickey, but, due to his circumstances, he was delighted to have the job, at least until something better came along.

After he'd been working for a few days, he came into a pub Chris and I were in, and was laughing his head off. He couldn't wait to tell us what had happened earlier in the day, and wasn't afraid to laugh at himself. Apparently, he'd been behind the bar in the pub when there were no customers in, and a couple of regular customers appeared outside and waved at him. So, being polite, he waved back. He was telling us between fits of laughter that these people then reappeared and waved again. So he waved back again. Then another guy appeared and also started waving. So our friend waved at him too. This went on for several minutes, until the owner suddenly appeared, ran past our friend, grabbed some stepladders and stretched up to the smoke alarm on the wall. The people outside had been waving at our friend to try to tell him that the alarm was ringing and to ask if everything was all right. Of course, he couldn't hear it – he's deaf. It's a good job there wasn't a real fire.

Unfortunately, the bar owners sacked our friend after two weeks, for no reason, and to this day he hasn't been paid a cent. Great Brits, eh?

Then there are the bar owners who are just taking the mickey. It wouldn't be allowed in the UK, but there are bars over here that increase their prices by the clock. There's a large pub on the seafront in Fuengirola where Chris and I went for a drink one afternoon shortly after we arrived in Spain. It was around 5.30 p.m., and I bought a pint of lager and a small shandy for Chris, which came to 4 euros 80 cents. We sat on the terrace in the sun and enjoyed our drinks.

'Shall we have another?'

'Why not?'

I went back to the bar and ordered the same drinks, and the barman asked me for an additional 1 euro 50 cents.

'But I've just had these same drinks and paid 4 euros 80 cents.'

'Yes, but we increase our prices at 6.00 p.m., again at 9.00 p.m. and then again at midnight.'

Not with me you don't pal. We walked out and never went back.

Town driving

The discipline is just not there when it comes to driving in Spain. Indicators – what are those? It appears that when you buy a new car in Spain, indicators must come as extras. Even on the odd occasion when the driver in front of you does use them, there's only a fifty/fifty chance that they're using them correctly, and you certainly can't assume that because they're indicating right, it means that they're intending to turn right. In fact, it's more than likely that they're actually planning to turn left.

You can be driving down a street in town when the car in front of you just stops, for no apparent reason. The driver will then get out and pop into the bakery for a loaf of bread. There isn't enough room to go round him, so you just wait until he comes out, gets back in his car and drives on. If you're new to Spain, you'll probably sit there blasting your horn, and the guy will just look at you as if you're mental. But you do get used to it, eventually. Stay loose; calm down. This is Spain. If it happened in the UK, people would be fighting in the streets, and the driver who'd stopped would finish up with his baguette wedged up his bottom.

What are synchronised traffic lights?
You can drive along virtually any road in any town in Spain and, as in the UK, there'll be a set of traffic lights at nearly every junction. The difference is that rather than being synchronised so that by the time you get to the next set they are at green and there's traffic flow, it's the other way around. Do they do it on purpose, just for a laugh? You get used to it and just take it for granted after a while, but there's no point in having more than two gears in your car when you're driving in town. The lights change, you take 20 seconds to put the car in gear and then crawl to the next set – there's no rush. The Spaniards have always lived here, so you'd think they'd get used to it as well. But no. There's Pedro Schumacher pulled up beside you in his completely illegal 1980's Seat Ibiza – and he's off. You then have to go even more slowly, because the view through your windscreen is obliterated by all the smoke coming out of his heap of junk. You'd get around quicker having someone walking in front of you with a red flag.

Look right, look left and then look right again?
Er, no! That's what you do in the UK. Don't forget that over here they drive on the other side of the road. So: on that basis it should be 'Look left, look right and then look left again' shouldn't it? Er, no again! There are two main reasons for this –

1)   Many drivers in Spain drive on the wrong side of the road in order to pass double parked vehicles, overtake on pedestrian crossings or just because they want to.

2)   Most one way streets are not actually acknowledged as one way streets by the local population. As such, it is bordering on the suicidal to look only one way if you are about to cross a one way street. Don't take anything for granted.

Look left, look right and then look left again. Then left, then right, then left, then right, then left, then right – then leg it as fast as you can!

Best before dates

If you pick up an edible product in a Spanish shop or supermarket, then whatever you do, check the 'best before date'. There will be a 'best before date' on the product somewhere, because it has to have by EEC law. However, don't be in the least bit surprised if this date has well gone. I don't know how they get away with it, or indeed if they are even aware that they are doing anything wrong. I have lost count of the times Chris and I have bought things in supermarkets or stores over here and then realized once we got them home that the 'best before date' had expired. There have been occasions when the product had actually already gone off, which would have meant that we could have expired had we eaten it. Sure, you can take it back if you bought it fairly locally, but if you do, the assistant will inevitably look at it, give you a blank look, shrug their shoulders as if to say 'What are you on about', and then walk away. Last year I bought a jar of Colmans English mustard from a supermarket in Fuengirola and then noticed a couple of days later that the 'best before date' had expired ten month earlier. I actually wrote to Colmans of Norwich explaining the situation and naming the store responsible. They never replied, so I guess they're not bothered either. It's an accepted fact that all of us are going to die at some point in time, none of us are going to get out of here alive, but dying from eating dodgy mustard wouldn't be my first choice.

What happened to all the car roof aerials?

Wherever you go on the Costas, you'll notice that virtually every car that should have a roof aerial hasn't got one. Where do they all go? It's a total mystery. Chris and I must have bought five replacements within our first six months here. If someone nicks a roof aerial, and that victim in turn nicks someone else's roof aerial, and so on, surely these objects would just travel around from car to car, wouldn't they? Apparently not. Someone must just walk around all day, every day, nicking roof aerials and then either eating or burning them. So where do they all go?

Walking on nutshells

When we used to arrive at our teashop each day, we could always tell if a Spaniard had been standing on our terrace the previous evening, because there were nutshells all over the place. They stand there with a bag full of these things, taking the tiny nuts out of the shells and then dropping the shells around their sandals. Irritating enough if the nut-eater had been alone, but if there'd been a few of them, the terrace would look like the floor of a very over-crowded aviary.

Scooters

The one thing that really does need sorting out in Spain is the scooter driver. The kids who drive these scooters are seriously crazy, and some of them don't appear to be any more than 13 or 14 years old. They cut you up, overtake on the inside, do wheelies on the seafront whilst overtaking, and drive on the pavements. It's not uncommon to see one driving a scooter whilst speaking into a mobile telephone and smoking a cigarette – at the same time.

Many of the scooters are obviously not roadworthy; in fact, they're complete wrecks. And hardly anyone wears a crash helmet. I thought Spain was subject to EEC law, but the police often appear to turn a complete blind eye to the lack of crash helmets. But it's not only the youngsters who are dicing with theirs and the lives of others: you'll often see a man on a large motorbike or scooter driving along without a crash helmet and with a toddler sitting in front of him, also with no head protection. What would happen if they ran into something or came off the bike doesn't bear thinking about.

The police in Spain really do need to start acting tough with these people. It's not as though they don't see it happening. Chris and I were once walking through Fuengirola when all of a sudden a number of police on motorbikes and in cars came down the road with horns blowing and blue lights flashing. They blocked the junction where we were standing and all the traffic ground to a halt. Something was happening, and it had a police escort.

We waited a couple of minutes and then this seemingly never-ending stream of motorcycles came through. It was a massive motorcycle rally, and most of the bikes were beautiful Harley Davidsons. Bearing in mind that the police were out in force, waving these bikes through each junction and providing motorcycle escorts on either side, it was quite extraordinary that most of the riders didn't have crash helmets on. Worse still, some of them had very young children with them, either straddling the petrol tank or just sitting in front of their (presumably) fathers. Some of these children were only three or four years old, and the police were completely ignoring it. Astonishing! In the UK, you'd be lucky to get 50 yards.

Glass curtains
Double-glazing, UPVC windows, call them what you want, the aesthetics and fit in Spain are way behind the UK standard generally. However, they do have these things called 'glass curtains'.

Because most people live in apartments on the Costa´s, and because it can get quite cold during the winter months, many people put glass curtains around their balconies in order to gain an extra room. They look fantastic – well, that's probably a bit misleading, because in fact you can hardly see them. They are sheet-glass panels, about half a metre wide with no frame, stretching from the top of the balcony to the floor. They fold back when it's warm, and they are brilliant: they look classy and are extremely functional.

But… There are people over here who seem to spend the best part of the day, every day, cleaning the bloody things. That amount of sheet glass takes some cleaning, and even when they are clean, they're never really clean. When you stand back to admire your work, there's always another bit that's got a mark on it.

It's easy to spot the glass-curtain owners in any urbanisation: they always have a window blade or squeegee in their hands. They might live on the top floor, but there they are, around the pool, looking up at their balcony clutching their blade. Then they shake their head, leg it back upstairs, appear on their balcony, do some more vigorous wiping, and then reappear at the pool a few minutes later.

However, in view of the above, you might be surprised when I say that I actually bought some glass curtains myself. I'd visited friends who have them around their balconies – floor to ceiling sheet glass panels that concertina back against the wall in summer and give you a beautiful conservatory during the winter – and I realised that they create another room. I'd asked around, and most people recommended a Finnish company, so I got them to do an estimate. It was all very professional, and once the Finnish sales manager had done all the measuring with one of those laser measuring devices, he sat me down and went through the specifications, timing, guarantee etc.

I'd decided that as well as having glass curtains around our balcony, I also wanted them around what in essence was a wasted space behind our kitchen, an area approximately 1 metre deep and running the full width of our apartment, but with no floor. The people below us, and many other owners on our complex, had already fitted a false floor in the equivalent area in their apartment, which they then used as a utility room. I wanted an office for writing, as I was using one of our bedrooms at the time, and realised that this would be the ideal use for the space.

No problem. The Finnish guy just leaned out of the window with his laser, took down the measurements, and off he went to generate a quote.

Although I'd more or less made up my mind that I was going to use the Finnish company, I also phoned a couple of other, British-owned, companies in order to get price comparisons and a feel for the competition.

The guys from the first company arrived in a clapped-out van, which didn't look as if it would make it to the nearest scrap yard. One of them was in his mid-twenties and the other was a totally disinterested teenager. They both looked as if they could do with a good wash, and although I know you shouldn't judge a book by its cover, I decided as soon as I saw them that there was no way I was going to use their company. They didn't know anything about the product, and it was perfectly obvious that their answer to every question I asked was a complete and utter guess.

Finally, they got out their tape measure. Although side to side measurements aren't too difficult when there are two people, it can be hilarious watching two people taking top to bottom measurements with a tape measure. The older of the two poked the loose end of the tape measure into the top corner of the roof and then dropped to his knees to secure the other end. But each time he got on his knees, the top of the tape measure would sway, bend and then drop on his head. Up he'd get again, with the same result. Although his colleague was trying to help, they didn't seem to be getting anywhere, and after five minutes of watching them as they appeared to be wrestling with a very determined boa constrictor, I had to retreat into a bedroom to laugh, while Chris disappeared onto the roof garden.

Obviously, they then had to guestimate the dimensions of the area behind the kitchen, as not even this pair were daft enough to try to go in there before a floor had been installed.

But then it was the turn of the guy from the other company, who arrived the next day wearing a well-worn chalk-striped suit in a temperature of about 85 degrees. He was pumping out perspiration and looked as if he was about to expire, but, in fairness, he was a really nice guy, if a little over-enthusiastic.

Once in our apartment, he immediately opened his briefcase whilst still standing, and all his papers and brochures fell out onto the floor. Gathering them up caused him to sweat even more profusely, but he carried on gamely and told me about the product.

'How long is the product itself and the workmanship covered under your guarantee?' I asked him.

'Five years normally,' he answered with a wink. 'But I'll have a word with my boss and he'll do it for ten years.'

'Oh, er, right then.' It didn't sound very professional. A guarantee's a guarantee, so was it for five years or ten years?

But off we went again with the measuring tape, which was jerking all over the place as if it had 10,000 vaults running through it. He was obviously keen to appear to have everything under control, and rather than ask me to hold one end of the tape measure for the side to side dimensions, he did it himself. I could see that the bow in the measure from one side of the balcony to the other equated to a good four or five inches, and that this measuring exercise was going to be anything but accurate. But, when he'd finished, I showed him the area that was going to be my office, opening the hall window so that he could stick out his head.

'Oh yes. No problem,' he said. 'I'll just climb out and measure it properly.'

I looked at him in surprise. 'You're having a laugh, aren't you? That's a false floor. The family below have already had a proper floor put in theirs, and what you can see there is basically sheet tin, which they've installed as a false ceiling. It's just tin plate painted white. It wouldn't take the weight of a cat.'

'No problem,' he continued confidently. 'I can walk around the edges on that wall.'

'Well, yes you could,' I said. 'I've done it myself in order to clean the windows. But for Christ's sake don't step off the wall onto the tin sheet. Anyway, why can't you just give me a guestimate, or come back later with a proper laser measure?'

But he was determined. 'No, that's not necessary. I don't let little things like that put me off doing the job.'

'Are you sure?' I persisted. 'Because it's potentially very dangerous if you get it wrong.'

'No problem,' he said again, and proceeded to climb out of the hall window onto the wall around the outside area.

I decided it was probably best to let him get on with it, and asked if he'd like a cup of tea.

'Yes please, that would be nice,' he replied. 'This won't take a minute.'

Suddenly there was the most horrendous noise – CRASH, BANG, SMASH – and my heart almost stopped beating.

'Oh God! Oh God,' I was muttering inanely as I ran to the hall window and looked down, dreading what I was going to see. There he was, sprawled out on the floor of the utility room below, surrounded by the pieces of a smashed plastic laundry basket and screaming and swearing as if he was about to die – which, looking back on it, he could well have been.

'It's my back, and my ankle, but particularly my ankle,' he wailed. 'I've f***** broken it, I'm sure. Get me out of here, quick! Oh shit! Oh shit! I've broken my f****** ankle.'

I was completely panic stricken.

'Quick, open this apartment door and get me out,' he called up pathetically.

'I don't have a key for that apartment,' I told him. 'And the owners only ever come down during August.' (It was April!) 'There are two options. Either you stay there until August and I lower a pork pie down to you from time to time, or I get a ladder from the garage and you climb up it.'

'How the f*** can I climb a ladder with a broken ankle?' he shrieked, which seemed a reasonable enough question.

'Right,' I said. 'I'll phone for an ambulance and they'll sort...'

'No, no, I don't want an ambulance,' he interrupted.

'There isn't an alternative. You can't stay there.'

'Can you lower your mobile down to me?'

'Well yes, I could, but I can phone the ambulance from up here.'

'I don't want to phone for an ambulance.'

'Well, who do you want to phone then?'

I swear, with my hand on my heart, that this is what he said next: 'I want to phone a friend.'

Well, that was it. I ran into the lounge, and Chris and I spent the next few minutes trying to suppress the sound of our laughter as we asked each other whether he'd be better asking the audience or perhaps going 50/50. It seemed awful to be laughing when the poor guy was obviously in agony, but we just couldn't help ourselves.

As soon as I was able to regain some self-control, I lowered my mobile phone to this guy and, sure enough, he phoned his friend. But apparently his 'friend' was too busy to come out, and told him he'd have to sort it out himself – some mate!

I could see that he was in genuine pain and that the time had come to take some action, so I phoned for an ambulance and then went down to the garage and brought the ladder up to the apartment.

The paramedics arrived within about ten minutes, and we all helped to bring the guy up into our lounge, where the senior paramedic confirmed that he had fractured his ankle and said that I should get him to hospital as soon as possible.

'Hang on a minute,' I said. You've got an ambulance. Aren't you taking him?'

'No,' the paramedic replied. 'We only deal with emergencies. You'll have to take him.'

Oh great! But they did help me get the guy down to my car, and I drove him the ten miles or so to the hospital in Marbella.

Needless to say, he didn't get the job!

Spanish companies and tradesmen

I've touched on this one before, when we required a plumber to unblock a drain in our teashop. I know for a cast iron fact that many Brits living in Spain would love to use Spanish companies or tradesmen. But the fact is that they are, generally speaking, totally unreliable. Punctuality and rushing are completely alien concepts to them. It's the culture (I think), and it will probably take them 10 or 20 more years to wake up to the fact that Brits don't like to wait. They'll pay for it, but they want it NOW. How these people are missing out.

I know the above probably sounds like the ranting of Basil Fawlty, but the truth is that if occasional irritation and annoyance are the payback for this great lifestyle, then it's a price I'm glad to pay.

Chapter 15
Lifestyle and cultural differences

I guess there must be people who don't particularly like the sun, but if you do, what a place this is to live. It's reckoned that the Costa del Sol gets on average 330 days of sunshine per year. That means you can actually plan to have a barbecue two weeks on Saturday and can almost guarantee that you'll be in the garden in the glorious sunshine having a fantastic time. In the UK, you could plan the same thing, invite some friends round, buy in the necessaries, and then finish up cooking it in the garage, pretending you're enjoying yourself. We've all done it, but what's the bloody point? You live inside in the UK, and that's the main difference from living over here.

For most of the year, we live outside. If you live in an apartment, the area that gets the most use is the balcony. You'll sit out there first thing in the morning with a cup of tea or coffee prior to going to work (if you work), then you'll sit out there in the evening to eat your meal. Inevitably, you'll also sit out there on your days off. People often spend more money on balcony furniture than they do on their lounge suite. The bigger the balcony, the better, and if you have a direct sea view, you've got the lot. It's as good as it gets.

Make sure you see the 'real' Spain
All too often, the Brits who live over here never get to see the real Spain. The Costa´s aren't the real Spain. I've lost count of the number of times I've heard people down here say things like, 'I'm sick of this place,' or 'I'm bored.' Okay, so get off your bum and do something about it then. You have to make the effort and drive inland in order to explore the real culture of the place – but it's there, so don't miss it.

We're lucky on the Costa del Sol, as a couple of hours driving at most will take you to some fantastic places. For me, one of the nicest places you can visit from here is actually also one of the nearest, Mijas

Pueblo. *Pueblo* means village, and that's just what Mijas is. Although the place has changed in that it now has numerous souvenir shops, restaurants and bars, you still get the Spanish village feel. As you enter Mijas Pueblo, there's a massive multi-storey car park, so finding somewhere to leave the car isn't a problem, and there's also an excellent regular bus service from Fuengirola.

There are three main levels to Mijas, and everywhere you go, you'll spot another tiny little street or a set of steps leading to somewhere or other. Don't get a guidebook; just wander. There are fantastic cafés, bars and restaurants, some of which are actually built into the cliffs. And the views are stunning: you look down on Fuengirola, which appears like a model village. Children love it too, as there are donkeys that are available for hire for a modest cost. Go there!

It's difficult to believe, but as you sit on the seafront in Benalmadena or Fuengirola during the height of winter, often in sunshine with the temperature 18 to 20 degrees C, you can see snow on the distant mountains of the Sierra Nevada. You can drive from brilliant sunshine to a ski resort in less than two hours – amazing. The last time Chris and I went up there, we set off in the Beetle dressed in shorts and T-shirts, and stopped in a lay-by halfway up the mountain to change into jeans and sweaters. Once we arrived at the ski village, we donned boots, another sweater, and thick coats – it was minus 5 degrees.

We took Dino with us, and he'd obviously forgotten what a British winter feels like, as he was walking on the snow as if it was broken glass, shivering and generally being a pain in the arse. We had a walk round, a cup of coffee (I wish they had Bovril), and then back to the car. If you like skiing, it must be great, but we don't, so we set off back to the coast. But instead of going back the way we came, through Granada, we dropped straight back to the coast near Nirja, and within an hour had stopped to put our shorts back on. The contrast in temperature is unbelievable.

You've got it all: from sunshine to skiing in an hour or so.

We once decided we wanted a few days' break from the teashop, so we took advantage of having our own business – and shut. It was a spur-of-the-moment thing during February, and I phoned the kennels to book Dino in and then we set off early the following morning on a three-day adventure. We took the donkey route (a really crap road) to Ronda, which cuts through the hills and mountains from Coin (pronounced Cohen). This is a fantastic drive, but much easier if you happen to be driving a half-track. You pass through stretches of countryside that are typically Spanish, and other areas that resemble Scotland or the Lake District. It's absolutely beautiful.

Being out of season, we had no problem booking into the big posh hotel in Ronda, right next to the gorge, which splits the town in half. We wandered around the town for the day, went to a Spanish restaurant for the *menu del dia* (menu of the day) and a couple of drinks (quite a lot of drinks actually), and then back to the hotel, feeling as though we were in 'proper Spain'. Then we got up the following morning and drove to Seville.

In many ways, Seville is like most cities around the world insofar as it's had bits added on to it over the years. But we wanted to stay in a hotel near the cathedral, in the original old city. Again, no problem with accommodation: it was only a two-star hotel but virtually new and very clean, with en suite – and right in the centre of the original old city. We checked in, had a quick shower and then went out for a walk. Similar to London, there are buses that go around the city passing numerous sights and buildings of interest. You can pick these buses up at various points and then get off to catch another one that takes a different route, which enables you to see something else you might be interested in. So we walked to the nearest pick-up point for a tourist bus and were amused by the fact that they were original old, open-top, right-hand drive London buses. How strange!

It was quite cold, so the coats were on again. Sod's law I guess, but we had no sooner got onto the bus than the heavens opened, and, as I think I might have mentioned before, when it rains in Spain it rains a lot. There we were on an open-top bus getting as wet as if we'd walked into the sea fully clothed.

There weren't many people on the bus – mostly Japanese tourists with ten cameras around their necks, and American tourists talking at the top of their voices, plus a few Brits. When it started to rain, everyone except the Brits disappeared to the ground floor. We were about as wet through as it's possible to get, but we were there for the views, and the views were what we were going to get. We switched routes and changed buses a couple of times and spent a good two or three hours being driven around in the pouring rain.

When we eventually got off, we stepped straight into the street, which was – no exaggeration – about three inches deep in water. If I'd spent ten minutes under a power shower, I couldn't have been wetter, and our feet were squelching big style. We were laughing, and the

Spaniards were giving us a wide berth and looking at us as though we were slap heads.

We had a street plan, and I guessed it was about a 20-minute walk to our hotel from the drop-off point. But it was a walk that would have been virtually impossible in that weather, so there was nothing for it but to head for the cathedral and try to find a café, or, as it turned out, a pub. Oh dear! We stayed there, out of the rain, until we'd downed about eleventeen strong Spanish beers, and eventually walked back out into the rain like a couple of hermit crabs.

We finally got back to our hotel, looking like the couple from a horror film who turn up wet and bedraggled at some remote and eerie hostelry in the middle of the night. With our squelchy shoes, water dripping off our hair and coats, giggling and walking sideways on rubber legs, we tried to ask the nice lady receptionist for the key in Spanglaise, which we thought was funny, although she obviously didn't.

Realising that we were in need of a *siesta* before facing the evening, we settled down for a quick nap – and were woken by light pouring in through the window the following morning.

The sight that greeted our eyes was reminiscent of the aftermath of a burglary, with everything spread all over the floor and clothes hanging off the wardrobe and over the shower rail, where we'd obviously spread them to dry, although we had no memory of having done so.

After a somewhat subdued breakfast, we paid the bill and left.

So all we can say is that we think it's nice in Seville, but we can't quite remember!

As we wanted to drive through the lakes on our way back to Fuengirola, we headed off the main motorway and into the beautiful surrounding countryside. The rain had stopped and we could have been driving through Scotland, but with sun. We pulled up in lay-bys a few times to take in the views and then went to a restaurant in El Chorro, which overlooks one of the lakes. We had the *menu del dia* again, while constantly urging each other to 'Look at that view', and then drove home after three days of wonderment – not counting the lost evening in Seville.

Fuengirola, Benalmadena, Nirja, Marbella and Puerta Banus are great for the tourist run, but do see the rest of Spain; it really is fantastic. Apart from Granada, Seville and Cordoba, there are lots of other places to visit and appreciate, and, when you've visited all of them, you can start on Portugal.

On one occasion, Chris and I decided to set off in the Beetle and travel up the Portuguese coast for a few days before returning home through the middle of Spain. On the return journey, we wanted to see as many little Spanish villages as we could, so we stayed away from the main roads and stuck to the country lanes. The Beetle's bilious colour and registration plate – AJO, which as previously mentioned means 'garlic' in Spanish – were enough to make Spanish people on the Costa's stare, so you can imagine the looks we got travelling through the *campo* (countryside) and passing through places where they hardly ever saw tourists.

On one of the many occasions when we got lost in the middle of nowhere, we came across a guy parked at the side of the road in a Mercedes. I stopped, explained the situation in very bad Spanish, and showed him my map, pointing out where we wanted to go. He stared wide-eyed at our car for a few moments and then started jabbering away at 90 miles per hour in Spanish, most of which went completely over my head. But I did manage to pick out what sounded like, 'Turn left after a couple of kilometres and then right.' So off we went again, and were back on track in no time.

We drove a further 110 kilometres that day and ended up in quite a large town called Zafra, which is quite near the Portuguese border, where we got into the one-way system and drove around in circles for a while. Finally, I spotted a hotel sign down a side street and, in my desperation to go anywhere rather than once more round the town, I veered straight across all the other traffic and shot down the side street, which was actually a very busy road. But, by sheer good luck, there was just one parking spot outside this hotel.

'I don't care what it's like or how much it costs,' I told Chris. 'I think we should stay here tonight.'

'If it's got running water, it's fine by me,' Chris agreed, exhausted as I was by the day's drive.

So we booked in, had a shower and got changed, and then went for a walk around the town. While we were out, we didn't see any restaurants that appealed, and we decided to go back and eat in the hotel restaurant. We'd ordered our meals and were sitting chatting when I suddenly felt a tap on my shoulder. 'Hola, Senor Cucaracha Amarillo,' said an amused voice – it was the guy in the Merc who'd given us directions 120 kilometres back up the road. 'I saw your car parked outside,' he said in broken English with an expressive shrug. How much of a coincidence was that then? You cant go anywhere in that car - perhaps it was time to get what he'd so aptly described as the 'Yellow Cockroach' re-sprayed.

The next morning, we set off again, making slow progress on some of the narrowest country roads I'd ever seen. Time was marching on, and when we hadn't found anywhere to stay by teatime, we were beginning to panic a little. Then, as we were driving through a small village about 50 kilometres north west of Seville, we noticed a roadside *venta* (café/bar) with a sign outside advertising rooms, so we pulled up and went inside to ask if they had a room available. The owner spoke very good English and told us that there were two rooms above the restaurant, and both were empty. Fine.

We were given a room key, but decided to have a quick drink at the bar before going upstairs, and the owner pulled us a couple of beers and gave us a small plate of green olives.

'These olives are absolutely beautiful,' I said. 'They're the best I've ever tasted.'

'Thank you,' the owner replied with a smile. 'They are from Antequera. They're in tins, so if you like them so much, I can sell you a tin.'

'That's great.' I said. 'Can you just add them to the bill?'

He disappeared into the backyard and then reappeared clutching what resembled a small dustbin with 'Antequera olives' printed on the front of it.

'Oh, er, thank you,' I mumbled, trying not to look surprised.

A few minutes later, he brought us another small plate containing what looked like very thin slices of cured ham drizzled with olive oil. I tasted a bit and it was absolutely fantastic, but obviously not ham.

'Ah, very special,' the owner said in response to my questioning. 'It's sun and smoke cured tuna steak. I can sell you a fillet vac packed if you like.'

'That would be great,' I said. 'Just add it to the bill' – along with the truck load of olives.

Next, he appeared with a plate of sliced cheeses, but I decided that however amazing they might be, enough was enough.

'This is goat's cheese,' he told us. 'And this is, er, how you say? Moo. And this one is chicken.'

Chicken cheese? I don't think so.

'Time to go,' Chris hissed at me. 'He's going to try selling us the entire bar if we don't leave soon.'

So, after a few minutes we managed to escape, and staggered up the stairs with our dustbin of olives, which weighed more than our suitcase.

After a shower, we had a quick walk around the village – which took about three minutes – and then went into the hotel restaurant for dinner. The owner showed us the menu and Chris ordered her meal. But I rather fancied some fish, so I asked him to translate the names of the fish that were on the menu. After telling me the more obvious ones, he suddenly disappeared, returning a little later holding a plate on which lay a huge, hideously ugly dead fish.

'This is very special and we are lucky to have it today,' he said proudly. 'It's a jabajaba.' (I can't actually remember the name.) 'You will have it and really enjoy it.'

'Oh, er, okay then,' I said, realising that I didn't really have any choice.

But he was right; our meal was beautiful, and, while we were drinking an after-dinner coffee, he returned for a chat. I asked him if he owned the *venta* himself and he confirmed that he did.

'It was built two years ago by local unemployed labour,' he explained. 'The council decided that there were too many unemployed people in this village, so they were set to work (men and women) building this place, which I then leased for 20 years.'

'Oh, that's good,' I said. 'But why were there so many builders, plumbers, electricians etc. unemployed at the time?'

'No, no no,' he said. 'It was built by unemployed olive pickers and pig farm labourers.'

I looked at Chris, trying to avoid letting my eyes stray around the room to check for signs that we might be about to fall through the floor or have the roof crash down on our heads.

The owner then went on to tell us that, as the following day was a Monday, there would be no one there when we left, as he closed on Mondays, and he asked if we could settle the bill before we went to bed and then let ourselves out via the fire escape in the morning.

'Are you being serious?' I asked him.

'Oh yes,' he said, obviously surprised that I should think otherwise. 'I will lock up when I leave tonight and if you could push the fire escape door open in the morning and go down the metal fire escape to your car, that would be fine.'

Er, I guess breakfast is out of the question then?

He disappeared, leaving Chris and me to concentrate on not thinking about Norman Bates, and then came back holding a very elaborate hat-type thing, which he placed on his head with a flourish. It resembled a straw boater, but was completely covered in brightly coloured paper flowers with ribbons hanging down about two feet around the brim. It looked like something that a particularly eccentric Morris dancer might covet, and I avoided looking at Chris, for fear that we would both erupt into hysterical laughter.

But the guy was oblivious to our discomfort. 'Once a year, a man from the village gets the privilege to wear this hat and sing a special song,' he said with pride.

'Oh, that's nice.'

'Yes,' he said, removing the hat from his head and holding it up against the wall. 'This would look very nice on the wall of your house. I will sell it to you if you like.'

Ten out of ten for sales effort, but no thanks.

'What about the music?' he continued, undaunted. 'This is a CD of the man in the hat singing his song at this year's fiesta.'

'No thanks,' I repeated, and he disappeared, leaving Chris and me time to recover our composure before following him out to the bar to pay the bill.

Next morning, we opened the fire door and descended the metal fire escape as instructed. The place was completely deserted, and we were relieved to drive away without having had to explain to the police what we were doing at the crack of dawn, creeping down the fire escape with suitcases and a dustbin full of olives.

See the real Spain. It's an experience.

The traditions

There's one thing that I admire above all about the Spanish people. Although they're part of the EEC, there's none of this 'we mustn't offend the minorities by flaunting our national traditions.' When they have a special day, it's a special day for them. If you want to watch, partake and be respectful, that's fine, but it is *their* day. They have countless saints' days as well as *ferria* weeks, which are during different weeks in different towns and are important to the locals. There's a fair ground, and the women and children dress in traditional Spanish costume, which they are proud of, and quite rightly so. There'll be horsemen and Flamenco dancers, and everyone will have a great time without getting completely legless.

Many towns, including Fuengirola, have an annual bull run, when wooden shutters are erected on both sides of the road from the bullring, around the block, and into a yard. I haven't measured it, but this run is probably only about 400 yards from start to finish, so it only lasts a few minutes. But it's a real spectacle. There'll be guys in fancy dress with running trainers or dressed as bull fighters, and amongst them will be the Brits in shorts and flip-flops, trying to look brave. Everyone waits for the doors to open and for the 'baby' bulls to run out along the bull run. They call them 'baby bulls', but they can outrun a Ferrari, and they don't look remotely like 'babies' close up. My advice is, if you have any sense, just watch.

New Year's Eve is also a great event in Spain. We went to the main church square in Fuengirola for our first New Year's Eve on the Costa del Sol, and it was brilliant. The council erected two stages and the pop groups and Flamenco dancers kept going all through the night. There's a tradition here that on the stroke of midnight you drink a glass of champagne and eat 12 grapes, one for each strike of the hour. I'd been forewarned of this, so I bought a bottle of bubbly and a bag of grapes and had taken 24 grapes, 12 for Chris and 12 for me. But I hadn't thought it through properly, because I'd bought grapes with seeds in them – and it isn't easy to eat one grape with seeds every second for 12 seconds. The square was packed with people and there we were, spitting and dribbling grape seeds and champagne all down our fronts and looking like complete idiots.

If you're ever in Spain when there's a *fiesta*, go to it. You will not be disappointed, and the local people will be delighted that you're interested.

Town rivalry

Oh boy; am I an admirer of Spanish town and city rivalry!

I guess you get town rivalry the world over to greater or lesser degrees. In the UK, the most noticeable element (and possibly the only one) of town rivalry is football, which often takes the form of 'my team is better than your team ner ner ner'.

In Spain, the football rivalry exists as it does in the UK, but by far the greatest form of town rivalry is roundabouts. Yes, that's right; roundabouts. Or; as they are called over here, 'rotondas'. It seems to me that many towns and cities in Spain must spend half of their annual budgets on roundabouts, and what the hell is wrong with that? I can think of worse things to spend people's council tax on can't you?

I don't know about where you live in the UK, but where I come from (West Yorkshire) there are basically two kinds of roundabouts. First of all there are the roundabouts with nothing on them whatsoever, and then there are the roundabouts which are full of beautiful flowers and a plaque or two stuck into the grass saying something like 'Sponsored by Albert Sprogett, Painter and Decorator' or, if it's a particularly large and highly elaborate roundabout, it might say something like 'Sponsored by Rodclunk plc'.

Not in Spain; oh no. Due to the lack of space in the centre of towns and cities you will as often as not see traffic lights at road junctions, but if there is the slightest chance to built a roundabout then that's it, and my oh my, do they have a field day or what. Statues, modern art, massive fountains and ginormous sculptures. The bigger and more flamboyant the better, and I think they're great. I am convinced that if Kracatoa was on the outskirts of Fuengirola they would build a road around it and declare it to be the biggest and the best roundabout in the world: 'Marbella – beat that then!' Each Town Council must have a massive 'Roundabouts Department' which does nothing else but design roundabouts and run on a bottomless pit budget.

I live near Fuengirola on the Costa del Sol, and Fuengirola council is well up in the premier league of roundabout building. The next town along the coast to the east is Benalmadena and they are well up there with them. A couple of years ago on the outskirts of Fuengirola, the council rebuilt a roundabout and as soon as all the brickwork was finished there was massive anticipation as to what would be built in the middle of this one as the existing ones would take a lot of beating. Would it be flower beds? Would it be palm trees? Would it be a fountain? No. Instead they erected a huge stainless steel exploding chocolate orange – wow! It looks like huge segments of an orange splayed out, and also vaguely resembles an opening flower-ish. Not satisfied with the exploding chocolate orange, they then started work on another roundabout only 2 or 3 hundred metres down the road from the exploding chocolate orange. Brickwork again, and then nothing for a month or two. Then, one day, guys arrived and started erecting this huge scaffolding in the middle of the roundabout and bit by bit, day by day, this mysterious shape began to appear. After a while they put large sheets over the scaffolding so that nobody could see the progress being made. What would it be? Nobody knew. Then, one day the scaffolding and sheets were removed and there it was – a huge man's torso with no head, no arms, no legs and no naughty bits. It's great, I love it. Then they started on another one on the main road to Benalmadena and they never seem to get short of new ideas. They had done the stainless steel bit and the classical sculpture type bit, so they must have thought they would now move on to a modern brightly coloured plastic looking type thingy. Bright turquoise and orange oddly sharp looking flame type shapes flying in all directions with the name 'Fuengirola', boldly spelt out in large orange letters in the middle of it. They're all fantastic and there is a huge one in Benalmadena which is full of little windmills spinning around continuously, and if they harnessed the power they could probably light up the whole town for free.

If there isn't enough room for a roundabout then inevitably they will built a huge structure over the road which is bigger than a footbridge. When you enter Marbella or Benalmadena you will go under one of these structures which have huge letters carved into them stating the name of the town. They want you know exactly where you are as soon as you get to the town limits. Bang! It's in your face and there can be no misunderstanding as to where you are. None of this little black and white sign at the side of the road business saying 'Welcome to soandso', or 'Soandso welcomes careful drivers', oh no, let's spend half a million euros on unashamed boldness which is bigger and better than those tosspots down the road have.

Town rivalry – it's great!

Spanish restaurants
Spanish restaurants and *ventas* (local bars) are marvellous. Shoot off into the hills and drop in at one of the thousands of *ventas* at the roadside, and you can enjoy a great meal in the sunshine for what you'd pay for two pints on the coast. They won't speak English, but they'll welcome you (in their own way). Swordfish, lamb cooked for so long that it falls apart as soon as you touch it, great local wine. Just relax. Well, try to relax. There'll probably be a few Spanish families at the tables around you, and although they'll all be shouting at each other as though they're about to start shooting each other, it's just a gentle conversation to them. Look at them, smile, put some earplugs in, and enjoy your meal.

Do you really want to go to Smelly Melly's for burger and chips?

'Gracias, por favor' – it's not necessary, or is it?

It's a British thing, and it's a nice British thing, it really is. Good manners, being polite, it's part of our culture, and I like it.

Common courtesy means a lot; and it tells people a lot about you. Saying 'please' and 'thank you' costs nothing. That's the way it should be, and it's the way most of us have been brought up. I used to get a smack round the back of the head if I didn't say it. Fair enough; it didn't do me any harm, as they say.

People come to Spain and sometimes think the Spanish serving them in shops and bars are ignorant because they don't get a *por favor* or a *gracias*. But it's not necessary most of the time; it's a different culture. I couldn't get my head round it initially, until we spoke one day to a Scottish lady who was married to a Spanish waiter. I can't remember how we got on to the subject, but she just laughed and said that her husband came in from the terrace on numerous occasions when she was waiting for him to finish his shift and said in Spanish, 'Christ, if those English people say "please" or "thank you" once more, I swear that I will strangle the bastards. Why do they keep saying "please" and "thank you"? I'm sick of it.'

So you see, it annoys us when they don't say it, and it annoys them when we do. Who's right and who's wrong? Nobody; it's just a matter of different cultures.

Dress

Forget the long trousers, socks, shoes and even your shirt. For most of the year, all these items of clothing are either hung up in the spare wardrobe or in a suitcase under the bed.

A pair of shorts and flip-flops – that's standard issue. Dress is one of many things in Spain that are totally irrelevant in terms of status. You don't judge someone on the way they dress. How can you? You can hardly make a fashion statement when you're wearing a pair of shorts and flip-flops. Okay, you may have a designer logo on one or both, but that means nothing here anyway, as you can buy rip-off designer gear at the local market for a few euros. It's a great leveller, because you may turn up at a barbecue wearing genuine, very expensive designer shorts, designer sandals and a Rolex watch, but I can say with a great deal of confidence that everyone else will assume that they're scammers from the local market or from one of the many Lookie Lookie men. So why bother?

The same goes for the ladies. There are, of course, certain ladies who will go the whole hog and dress completely over the top, with a posh frock, gold shoes and a gold handbag. But once at the party or barbecue, you can see them gradually becoming more and more uncomfortable. A nice pair of sandals, a thin skirt and bikini top or a thin cotton dress, that's all you need, and generally speaking that's the way it is here. You save a fortune on clothes because you don't actually need many.

Cars

There's a saying over here, 'Never judge anyone by the car they drive.' The reason for this is that it's completely pointless having a decent car. Even if you do have one in immaculate condition, it won't stay that way for very long.

When we first arrived in Spain in our hairdresser's Beetle, there was not even a hairline scratch on it. After we'd been here for about a week, we returned to the car one day and there was a bash on the corner of the rear colour-coordinated bumper.

'Oh hell! No! Who's done that? What a bastard.' I was distraught. Like most men, I've always taken great pride in our cars: I was the one on the drive every Sunday with the car wax, T-Cut, upholstery cleaner...

A short while later, there was another knock on the front bumper, and at the end of our first year, the car resembled the Bluesmobile, apart from the silly colour. In no time at all, I was into the Spanish way: 'Oh the car's been whacked again,' I'd say with a shrug of the shoulders, before getting into it and driving off.

The next time you're in Spain, look at the rear of cars, and you'll see tow bars, thousands of them. Get one! A tow bar is a must-have accessory, far more useful than indicators, as any Spaniard will tell you. For the Spanish, parking is somewhat of a hobby. They reverse in and whack the car behind with their tow bar, pull forward and touch the car in front, and then reverse into the centre of the space. Easy. Parked. That's it. Job done.

We know some seriously rich people over here who drive cars with knocks all over them. It's not worth going and getting it fixed, because you can put money on it that it will have been whacked again within a couple of weeks. So that's another money saver. In the UK, it's the done thing to change your car every two or three years, and if it gets knocked, it's straight into the garage for a re-spray – you can't be driving about in a car looking like that, can you?

There is no status symbol associated with cars over here.

If you fancy a drink

Alcohol is a funny thing. It's part of our culture in Britain to go out and get as pissed as possible in as short a period of time as possible. Things may have changed a little since the relaxation of pub opening hours, but the culture is still alive. You work hard, so you play hard, especially on Friday and Saturday nights – I certainly did. But in Spain there has never been a problem getting a drink, and it's much, much cheaper here. So the Spanish have never had to get as much down their necks as possible in the quickest possible time. As often as not, they'll have a coffee and then enjoy a couple of glasses of wine with their evening meal.

You'd be amazed at the places where you can get an alcoholic drink. For instance, shortly after we arrived in Fuengirola I took our Beetle to the local VW garage for a service. As agreed, I went back to collect the car later in the day and it wasn't quite ready. While waiting, I noticed one of the mechanics coming out of the workshop to a vending machine in the office and buying a can. Out it rolled, and I did a double take – it was a can of beer. They had a vending machine selling mineral water, soft drinks, and beer – in a garage. Can you imagine that in the UK? There'd be mechanics falling all over the place, writing cars off by the dozen.

Also, you can walk into a McDonalds in Spain and order a Big Mac and eleventeen beers. What more could you want?

Even the cafeteria in the Costa del Sol Hospital in Marbella is really a bar. Patients probably wonder why, after a few minutes' polite conversation, their Brit visitors say irritably, 'Ooh, it's hot in here. I think I'll just go for a wander round', and then they never see them again. If you walk into the hospital's cafeteria, you can spot the Brits immediately. There'll be Spanish families with sandwiches and coffee or doughnuts and bottles of coke, and then there are the tables littered with beer bottles. Guess who? Can you imagine a hospital bar in the UK? I don't think so, do you?

One secret haven for many Brits over here is the petrol station, most of which, particularly the large ones on major roads, have bars attached to them and are open 24 hours a day. That's right, you can drive in at 4 o'clock in the morning, fill up, and down six pints. But it's worth remembering that the beer over here is much stronger than that in the UK: a standard lager in the UK is about 4%, whereas over here it's 5.5% to 5.6%.

There's one of these petrol stations quite near our house, and on the odd occasion when we've been out to a party or a club, we'll get the taxi to drop us off there for a nightcap. And we're in good company, because some of the best customers in these petrol station bars during the night are the police, having a nice whiskey or two before they drive off into the night.

Prepare to be visited by all your 'mates'
You find when you move to Spain that all of a sudden some people you knew (not particularly well) in the UK miss you dreadfully. Family and close friends visit you and it's terrific to see them. But then there are the people who phone or e-mail telling you that 'It would be great to see you again and we were thinking of coming over for a week.' Yeah right. Rough translation: 'We thought we'd pay for a cheap flight and get a free holiday.' It's an amazing fact that when you say to these people, 'Yes that would be great. I'll look around and see what it would cost you to get an apartment to stay in,' the answer is usually a somewhat less enthusiastic, 'Oh, right, yes, of course' – and then they tend not to come.

We have family and close friends over to visit regularly, and it really is a pleasure to see them and to have them staying with us. We've all got each other's range now, but to start with everyone who visited us thought we were on holiday as well.

'Where shall we go tonight then? Do you fancy a Chinese? And then we could go to a bar where they have live entertainment. On Sunday we could shoot up into the mountains and have a meal at a nice little Spanish restaurant. Ronda, we haven't been there. I've heard it's really nice. Can we go there as well?'

When you have to get up for work the following morning, the last thing you want to do is go to some music bar until daft o'clock and get completely pissed on loopy cocktails. If you're on holiday, fair enough, but we aren't. It didn't take us long to start telling visitors in the nicest possible way that it would be far easier and better if they hired a car so that they could do their own thing some of the time.

In the beginning, we had people staying with us who never dipped into their pockets once. They emptied the freezer, the cupboards and they drank all my beer! We'd work all day and then get home to a bowl full of washing up, and start cooking again while they lay on sun loungers on the balcony. I call that taking the piss.

So beware of the mates you forgot you had.

'No win, no fee' – never heard of it

It's unlikely that you'll ever hear those words over here. Visit anywhere along the Costa´s and there's building work going on. Roads are constantly being dug up, pavements changed to accommodate parking bays, and massive craters appearing that will eventually be underground car parks. You struggle to drive into Fuengirola two days running without some road or other being closed and the traffic being diverted in another direction – usually not the one you want to go in. Wherever you go, there's something being dug up, and the Spanish are far from organised when it comes to coning off or the segregating areas where you can and cannot walk.

It's very difficult for older people in particular, but, surprisingly enough, the Spanish just seem to take it in their stride and get on with it. In the UK, there'd be people falling over in droves, armed with cameras, and getting straight on the blower for compensation. Over here, things don't work like that. If you fall over, speak to someone at the town hall or the police and you'll get the same answer: 'You should watch where you're going.' And that's fair enough; I don't have a problem with that.

Political correctness

There's been a lot of publicity about racism in Spanish football, and that can't be right. Overall, however, political correctness is not something that exists in everyday Spanish life. You can't say this, you can't do that – of course you can. The Spanish just do what they've always done. They are quite rightly proud of their history and traditions, and nobody is going to start telling them to change.

The one solitary example I saw of an attempt at political correctness had me in stitches. For years along the seafront in Fuengirola there were very large, skip-sized plastic bins on wheels. Bar and restaurant owners would put their rubbish into these after a day's work, ready for the bin men to empty during the night. Then, one day, workmen arrived opposite our teashop and started digging a bloody great hole in the pavement. This hole got bigger and bigger, and eventually they lowered large metal bins into it, which were on hydraulic elevators. They were to be our new underground bins, and the eyesore plastic skips would be taken away. This was a great move, and would certainly improve the aesthetics of the promenade. Once all the bins and hydraulics were in place, they then put huge lids on them. There were three funnels coming out of each lid, which were, in effect, chutes for the rubbish to go down into the relevant bin. One was for any household and perishable waste, one for paper and the third was for plastic material.

Once the work was finished, I went across to look at these new chutes and there, on each one, was a sign highlighting the type of rubbish you could put down it – and underneath the graphics was another large sticker in Braille. These chutes were actually sticking out of the pavement with no protective barrier. The only way a blind person would know that they were there was when they fell over one. But I suppose at least they could then feel the sticker and know if they'd fallen over the plastic chute or the household waste chute.

The farmacia (chemist)

Things are no doubt different inland at the small towns and villages, but, generally speaking, in the major resorts along the Costa´s the *farmacias* are brilliant. Most speak perfect English and almost act as doctors. As with anything, some are better and friendlier than others, but in most cases you can explain your problem and they are more than willing to give you advice and prescribe the necessary drugs or medicines. If you had a serious ailment, you'd be well advised to go to a doctor or to the hospital, but the *farmacias* are as good as many British GPs.

What about the prices of drugs and medicines? They are generally much cheaper here than in the UK and, in certain instances much, much cheaper. I wonder how that can be, when the UK has the National Health Service, but I've been astonished on many occasions at how little certain medications cost, and some tourists actually buy pharmaceuticals in bulk to take home.

The vet

As with the *farmacias*, the vets here are great. I obviously can't comment on all of them, but the ones we've used have been absolutely fantastic. Many speak perfect English, are very helpful and don't rush you. People who move abroad and bring their pets with them worry about veterinary care just as much as they do about their own medical care – don't.

168

I have a serious phobia: hypodermic needles. Show me one and I'm gone; I'll hit the floor in less than a second. I even passed out in the hospital when my son Oliver was born. I was okay with the actual birth, but when a nurse advanced towards my wife with a hypodermic needle, I woke up in the hospital corridor with my head between my legs and a voice telling me to take deep breaths. You may be wondering what this has got to do with vets, but stick with me.

We've taken Dino to the vet on numerous occasions for various reasons, but during one visit the vet picked up a package that I knew contained a needle.

'Wooh, stop there! If you get that out now, I'm a gonner.'

'No problem. Just go outside and I'll call you back in when I've finished,' he said.

Sure enough, a couple of minutes later, the vet called me back in, sat me down and proceeded to tell me that for many years he'd had a serious phobia with elevators, and that he had sympathy with my situation.

'Have you had therapy?' he asked.

'Well no, but then I'm not actually insane. I just don't like needles.'

He went over to the cabinet, took out two brand new hypodermic needles, still in their packets, and gave them to me.

'That's a start,' he said. 'When you feel that you can do it, open the packets and just handle the needles. That's all. It may help you.'

How nice can you get? He didn't have to do that. Unfortunately, though, I'm still shit scared of needles.

Some time after that incident, Dino developed a serious skin infection and was put on a course of tablets. But his condition didn't improve, so the vet put him on another course of injections and took various blood samples, which had to be sent away to a laboratory in Barcelona. Poor old Dino; he was 16 years old and looked in a hell of a state. It was bad enough that he was deaf and half blind due to cataracts, but now he had big lumps of fur missing and looked a really sorry sight.

His illness coincided with our plan to go on holiday to Portugal in the car, and there was nothing else for it but for us to cancel. There wasn't a kennel in the whole wide world that would have taken Dino looking like that.

Then, on one of our visits to the vet for Dino's injections, I mentioned the fact that we were cancelling our holiday because of his condition, and the vet didn't even hesitate. 'Oh, don't do that. I'll look after Dino for you. In fact, the timing is perfect, as the lab results will be here whilst you are away, and I can begin his treatment myself in your absence.'

Now how nice is that again? This veterinary surgery is in Fuengirola, and the vet's name is Jesus, which is not an uncommon name in Spain, and pronounced 'Hésuse'. What a guy!

On top of all that, the vets over here charge only a fraction of what vets in the UK charge.

While on the subject of dogs, if you've recently moved to Spain or are considering doing so and you're a dog lover, you will either have brought your own dog over with you or you may be planning to buy or adopt one over here. I hope that you'll already feel encouraged by what I've said about Spanish vets, but you may be wondering what you're going to do with your dog when you want to go back to the UK to visit family and friends.

Wherever you look in Spain, you'll see stray dogs, dogs locked on balconies for hours on end, dogs tied up with a piece of old rope; it's generally a sad state of canine affairs. But don't get me wrong; you'll also see lots of Spanish people walking around proudly with Yorkshire terriers or little Peekawotsit thingies with ribbons in their hair. However, when it comes to mixed-breed five-bob dogs, they are usually on the street, although it would be unfair to blame the Spanish alone for this situation, as some of the main culprits in the coastal resorts are the Brits themselves. People move over here from the UK and before they know what's happened, they've adopted or purchased a dog or cat. Sometimes (quite often), things don't work out as they planned, and sometimes, out of desperation, they abandon the animal. Some people book their dog or cat into kennels for a week, leg it to the airport for a plane home, and never return, and many of these animals are then taken in by other Brits or by British-run animal sanctuaries, and these people do a brilliant job. For instance, there's a privately run British animal charity in Fuengirola called PAD (Protección de Animals Domésticos), which, in eight years, has found new homes for more than 5,000 dogs and cats.

If you live somewhere near the coast of Spain – and that's where most Brits choose to live – there will be at least one British or Scandinavian kennel/cattery. It seems an obvious thing to say, but make sure you visit the place first, rather than just booking your dog in over the phone from an advertisement you saw in a newspaper. You'll usually find that the price is reasonable and that the place is extremely good and compares very favourably with the kennels you've used in the UK.

So, if you think you'd like to move to Spain but concerns about your dog's welfare are preventing you from doing so, you can rest assured – the vets are good and the kennels are good.

The Carretera

This is the dual carriageway that runs along the coast of the Costa del Sol. It's a racetrack without rules; pure Mad Max stuff. Anything goes: overtaking, undertaking, tailgating to the extent that the driver might as well sit on the back seat of the car in front – come to think of it, that's where some of them finish up. Bumps, pile-ups, multiple shunts are all just part of the tale of everyday folk for users of the Carretera. You think it's crazy on the M25, M1 or M62? Believe me, they're tame by comparison. People in Mercs go for gaps here that you wouldn't dare go for in a Smart Car in the UK. It's a complete shambles.

They built a beautiful new motorway on the Costa del Sol about a kilometre inland to take volume traffic off the Carretera, but they charge people for using it. Result: nobody uses it; it's completely empty. There's no charge on the stretch from Malaga to Fuengirola, and that bit's packed; but if you carry on after Fuengirola, you think the world has ended and nobody thought to tell you. You can drive for miles and not see another vehicle until you get to the first tollbooth at Calahonda, where you have to wake up the attendant.

Chris and I were driving along the Carretera one day when a car seemed to come up behind us from nowhere with its headlights on full. I thought at first that it was the police, but for some reason the car slowed down when it got level with me and then cut straight across the front of our car. I slammed on the brakes to avoid yet another bash on the front wing, and this car then sauntered on in front – which is when I noticed an L plate in the rear window. He or she was a learner, and presumably the guy teaching had told them to slow down, which they took rather too literally.

'Look at that,' I said to Chris. 'He's a learner and his L plate is upside down.'

'Well yes,' said Chris. 'But it'll be the right way up further along the road when the car's on its roof.' Good answer.

To be fair, when there is an accident on the Carretera, or anywhere else for that matter, the police have the traffic moving in a fraction of the time it would take in the UK. These guys don't mess about measuring tyre marks or listening to arguments about whose fault it was. Out comes the whistle – the Spanish police love their whistles – and an electric bright-light baton. They'll bounce a car out of the way if necessary, but their first priority is to get that traffic moving again – quickly.

The Carretera: not for the faint hearted.

Speedboats

If you live down here, at some point you'll inevitably think to yourself, 'I fancy a speedboat.' You sit on the promenade or on the beach and see these things going past, and you can't help wanting one. In fact, you can buy a nice second-hand speedboat relatively cheaply, for about the price you'd pay for a mid-range car. But be careful. It's one thing buying a boat, but it's quite another thing getting it into the water. You can't just drive down onto the beach and launch a boat at the water's edge; you require a birth in a harbour, and that's expensive.

Chris's son, Jonathan, had a speedboat that he moored in Cabopino Port, which is between Fuengirola and Marbella. During the summer, it cost him 500 euros per month just to have it sitting in the water. That's the price of a small mortgage! He went out in it periodically, but once you get to the mouth of the harbour, it's a case of, 'Shall I turn left or right?' Then you drive/ride for a while (I'm not sure whether you drive or ride a speedboat), but it doesn't take long before you think, 'I'm bored now,' and take it back to its mooring. The novelty doesn't generally last very long, and people sell them on within a few months. Sounds great; isn't.

The things you miss

It's true to say that there is very little you cannot now buy along the Costa's. The difference is that in the UK you can go into virtually any supermarket and get whatever you want in one hit. Over here, you'll have to go to one particular shop for one product you're after, and another shop for something else. So it can be a day's job doing the shopping if you want specific British produce and brands.

Different people like different things, and some British people who live here are quite happy to settle for Spanish products altogether, without requiring anything else – but not many.

The following are some of the things I miss.
Our UK family. That goes without saying.

Gala pie. For anyone who's never heard of Gala pie, it's a large slab of pork pie with boiled eggs running through it. I'd risk prison for a slice of that with brown sauce on it.

Marzipan fruits.

My best mate Norman. I miss him a lot (in a manly kind of way). Chris doesn't miss him, as she thought he led me astray. Funny that; his wife Jackie won't miss me, as she thought it was *me* who led *Norman* astray!

My local pub. 'The Brown Horse' in Coley near Halifax. I love living here, but hardly a Sunday lunchtime goes by when I don't think to myself, 'I wish I was there now, just for an hour.'

The Karachi on Neil Street in Bradford – now *that's* a curry house.

Jokes. They're part of everyday office and shop-floor life in the UK. Hardly a day used to go by without someone coming out with a new joke, sometimes good, sometimes bad. You just don't get good jokes here.

Gardens. I love gardening. I really, really love gardening. I had a huge garden in the UK and spent every spare moment just pottering about in it. I could get home late from work, be really stressed, and Chris would put a gin and tonic in my hand and I'd wander about in my garden. Ten minutes later, and I was okay. I was by no means an expert gardener, but I like to think that my garden was the best in the whole world. It was to me anyway.

Now I feel as though I've had an arm amputated. I walk out onto our balcony or up onto our roof terrace and there's no garden. The roof terrace is huge and it is a kind of garden, but, instead of grass, there are ceramic tiles and terracotta pots. You can grow things in pots until hell freezes over but it's not the same – and there's not much use for a Hayter petrol mower on a roof terrace.

I've tried to create a little England and failed, many times. I spend a fortune on seeds, bulbs, compost, and what do I get? Dead plants. With intense heat and salt from the sea air, you don't stand a chance.

Our urbanisation has beautiful communal gardens, but they're not mine. Sack the gardener; I'll do it for free.

Proper Cling Film. The Spanish can't make proper Cling Film: the stuff they make is film, but it doesn't cling; it's more like a plastic bag on a reel. There's a huge market out here in Spain just waiting for a British Cling Film manufacturer. Everybody wants it. Pack it in a box printed with a huge Union Jack design on it and call it 'PROPER cling film'. Please!

Chris and I talk a lot about what we miss, and she misses different things. I asked her what would be the first things she'd buy if she walked into a UK supermarket. 'A metal potato masher and a pair of oven gloves,' she said. Oh right. I can't say they're things I'd have thought of.

'Okay Chris, but what do you miss most about the UK?'

'The spring lambs jumping around in the fields in Yorkshire.'

I can't say that's something I'd have thought of either.

'The things you miss' is often also a topic of conversation in our local bar, and the diversity of the feedback is surprising.

'Being at Old Trafford on a Saturday afternoon. Some bastard's sat in my seat.'

'Thornton's chocolates.'

'Being indoors with fitted carpets and the central heating on full during a really cold winters day.'

Eh? Are you mad?

If you want British brands of particular items, the chances are that you'll pay through the nose for them – when you can get them.

The things I don't miss

Top of the list has to be traffic and long faces. Before I left the UK, I could do upwards of 50,000 miles a year. On a typical day, I'd get up in the morning and drive from near Halifax to Slough and back, or to Glasgow and back, and think nothing of it. As I mentioned earlier, for the last three years of my working life I commuted from near Halifax to Hinckley in Leicestershire – that's a 240-mile round trip. I loved the place and the people, but not that much. I was like a robot.

When we do go back to the UK to visit family and friends, I'm immediately gob-smacked as soon as I drive our hire car out of the airport. Where are all these people going? Where do they all live? Is there enough room? You probably don't notice it, as I certainly didn't when I lived there, but stand back from it for a while and take a look. It's lunacy.

And what's happened to Sundays? They were the quiet days when you washed the car, cut the grass – oh yes, and went to the pub at lunchtime. But not now. I'm sad when I'm in the UK on a Sunday; it's not the same. The M62 seems to be just as busy on a Sunday as it is during the week, and there are massive queues of cars waiting to get into those out-of-town shopping centres. People seem to feel they have to go out and cheer themselves up by purchasing a new three-piece suite, which they don't really need and probably can't afford.

Whenever I go back to the UK, everyone seems to be miserable. Before we moved to Spain, Chris's son used to say the same thing to us when he visited the UK, and I found it quite offensive. What does he mean? I'm not miserable. But I probably seemed it to him. But over here, most of the people we meet are holidaymakers, so I guess we see them at their best, and therefore it's probably unfair to make a direct comparison.

In summary

When Chris and I came over here, we didn't know anything about anything and, not surprisingly, we made some mistakes and could have done some things better. We've seen a number of sad cases of people who didn't do their homework and didn't think things through, and their dream life in the sun turned into a nightmare. Some of the disasters were due to innocence, and others to sheer stupidity. You cannot move to Spain and permanently play at being on holiday unless you have a never-ending supply of money, which few people have. If you get it right, you'll never look back, and you'll wonder why you didn't make the move years ago. However, if you get it wrong, failure and disillusionment will be the order of the day.

If I could pick one statement out of the whole of this book to offer as a seminal piece of advice, it would be this one:

'...just assume that everyone is out to rob you and you can then be pleasantly surprised when you find that they're not.'

If you enjoyed reading this book, try 'Leeds fans on holiday' which is also available on Amazon Books.